Barney E. Warren, Andrew L. Byers

Songs of the Evening Light

For Sunday Schools, Missionary and Revival Meetings and Gospel Work in General

Barney E. Warren, Andrew L. Byers

Songs of the Evening Light
For Sunday Schools, Missionary and Revival Meetings and Gospel Work in General

ISBN/EAN: 9783337270490

Printed in Europe, USA, Canada, Australia, Japan

Cover: Foto ©Thomas Meinert / pixelio.de

More available books at **www.hansebooks.com**

SONGS

OF THE

EVENING LIGHT

FOR

SUNDAY SCHOOLS,
MISSIONARY AND REVIVAL MEETINGS
AND
GOSPEL WORK IN GENERAL.

EDITED BY

Barney E. Warren and Andrew L. Byers.

✦✦✦✦

Published by
GOSPEL TRUMPET PUBLISHING CO.,
GRAND JUNCTION, MICH.

PRICES: Single Copy, postpaid, 35 cts.; Per Dozen, $3.60.

PREFACE.

We are in the evening of the last dispensation of time. In fulfillment of the prophecy—"At evening time it shall be light."—(Zech. 14 : 7.) The pure gospel is shining now as it never has shone since the days of primitive Christianity. The ransomed of the Lord are returning from their apostatized condition and are coming "to Zion with songs and everlasting joy upon their heads." As the brilliant light of full salvation shines within us, and we realize that we are given "power over all the power of the enemy," enabling us to live free from all sin, it starts the well-spring of holy song within our souls; and thus, "SONGS OF THE EVENING LIGHT" appropriately expresses its own meaning.

So far as our limited ability and time have allowed, we have taken great pains and care in arranging this collection, and we gratefully acknowledge the help of the Lord. While we do not pretend to cope with skilled music writers, we are glad that the more artistic music is not necessary to the divine inspirations and influences that attend songs that are sung "in the Spirit;" and we believe that these songs are such as will be blessed in this manner.

Scattered throughout the book will be found a few songs from some of the well known writers, and others, whom we thank for their kindness in permitting us to use them.

With the exception of these last named, and a few taken from *Echoes from Glory*, the songs in this book are nearly all new. Those taken from *Songs of Victory*, and *Anthems from the Throne*, are new except to a very few people.

This cllection contains songs suitable for almost every kind of gospel service, and includes a number suitable for children's meetings.

As we are young in experience in this work, we hope to be excused for whatever defects may be found in the book. Those who are gifted on this line should let God use them in composing spiritual songs, so that when a new book is needed, there will be plenty from which to select, thus avoiding a hurried compilation.

We send out SONGS OF THE EVENING LIGHT with an earnest prayer that its hymns may bring many souls to Christ, and that it may work an important part in this great and last reformation. Amen.

THE EDITORS.

Copyright, 1897, by The Gospel Trumpet Pub. Co.

MEREDITH, MUSIC PRINTER, CHICAGO.

What a Kingdom! Concluded.

saves from all sin, And 'twill last while the a-ges shall roll.

No. 5. Open Wide the Door.

B. E. W.   (Rev. 3:20)   B. E. WARREN.

1. Sin-ner, hark! the Saviour's call-ing, Plead-ing o'er and o'er;
2. Wea-ry sin-ner, lost and sigh-ing, Hear the call *once more;*
3. Wake the joy for-e'er in-creas-ing, On that bliss-ful shore;
4. Hear the Gos-pel message giv-en; Bar it out no more;

Hear those ten-der ac cents fall-ing: "O-pen wide the door."
See the Sav-iour bleeding, dy-ing; O-pen wide the door.
Give thy-self in Je-sus' keep-ing; O-pen wide the door.
Christ will speak thy sins for-giv-en; O-pen wide the door.

CHORUS.

Hum-bly bow with broken spir-it, Heaven's mer-cy to im-plore;

Je-sus calls, O sin-ner, hear it! O-pen wide the door.

No. 6.   Trust and Obey.

J. H. SAMMIS.   BY PER. D. B. TOWNER, OWNER OF COPYRIGHT.   D. B. TOWNER.

1. When we walk with the Lord In the light of his Word, What a glory he sheds on our way! While we do his good will, He abides with us still, And with all who will trust and obey.
2. Not a shadow can rise, Not a cloud in the skies, But his smile quickly drives it away; Not a doubt nor a fear, Not a sigh nor a tear Can abide while we trust and obey.
3. Not a burden we bear, Not a sorrow we share, But our toil he doth richly repay; Not a grief nor a loss, Not a frown nor a cross, But is blest if we trust and obey.

CHORUS.

Trust and obey, For there's no other way To be happy in Jesus But to trust and obey.

4 But we never can prove
The delights of his love
Until all on the altar we lay;
For the favor he shows,
And the joy he bestows,
Are for all who will trust and obey.

5 Then in fellowship sweet
We will sit at his feet,
Or we'll walk by his side in the way;
What he says we will do,
Where he sends we will go,
Never fear, only trust and obey.

No. 9. Come, Sinner, Come.

E G. M.   (Rev. 22:17.)   E. G. MASTERS.

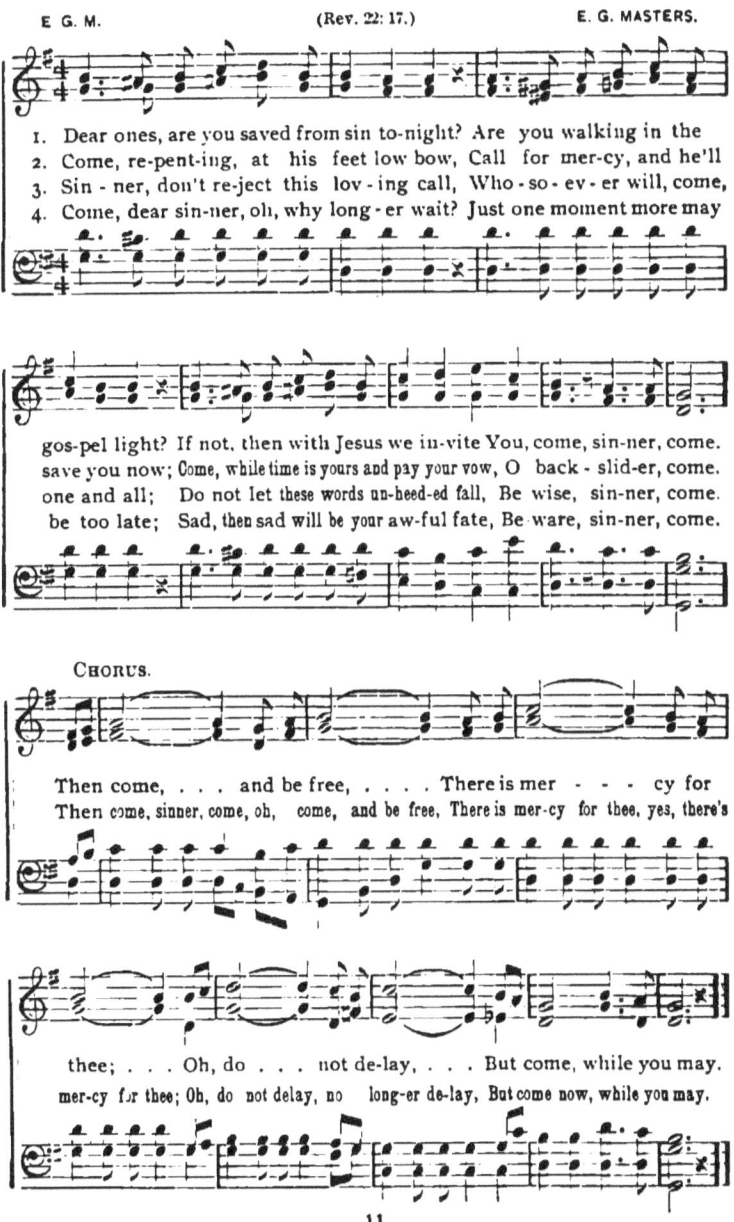

1. Dear ones, are you saved from sin to-night? Are you walking in the
2. Come, re-pent-ing, at his feet low bow, Call for mer-cy, and he'll
3. Sin-ner, don't re-ject this lov-ing call, Who-so-ev-er will, come,
4. Come, dear sin-ner, oh, why long-er wait? Just one moment more may

gos-pel light? If not, then with Jesus we in-vite You, come, sin-ner, come.
save you now; Come, while time is yours and pay your vow, O back-slid-er, come.
one and all; Do not let these words un-heed-ed fall, Be wise, sin-ner, come.
be too late; Sad, then sad will be your aw-ful fate, Be ware, sin-ner, come.

CHORUS.

Then come, . . . and be free, ... There is mer - - - cy for
Then come, sinner, come, oh, come, and be free, There is mer-cy for thee, yes, there's

thee; . . . Oh, do . . . not de-lay, . . . But come, while you may.
mer-cy for thee; Oh, do not delay, no long-er de-lay, But come now, while you may.

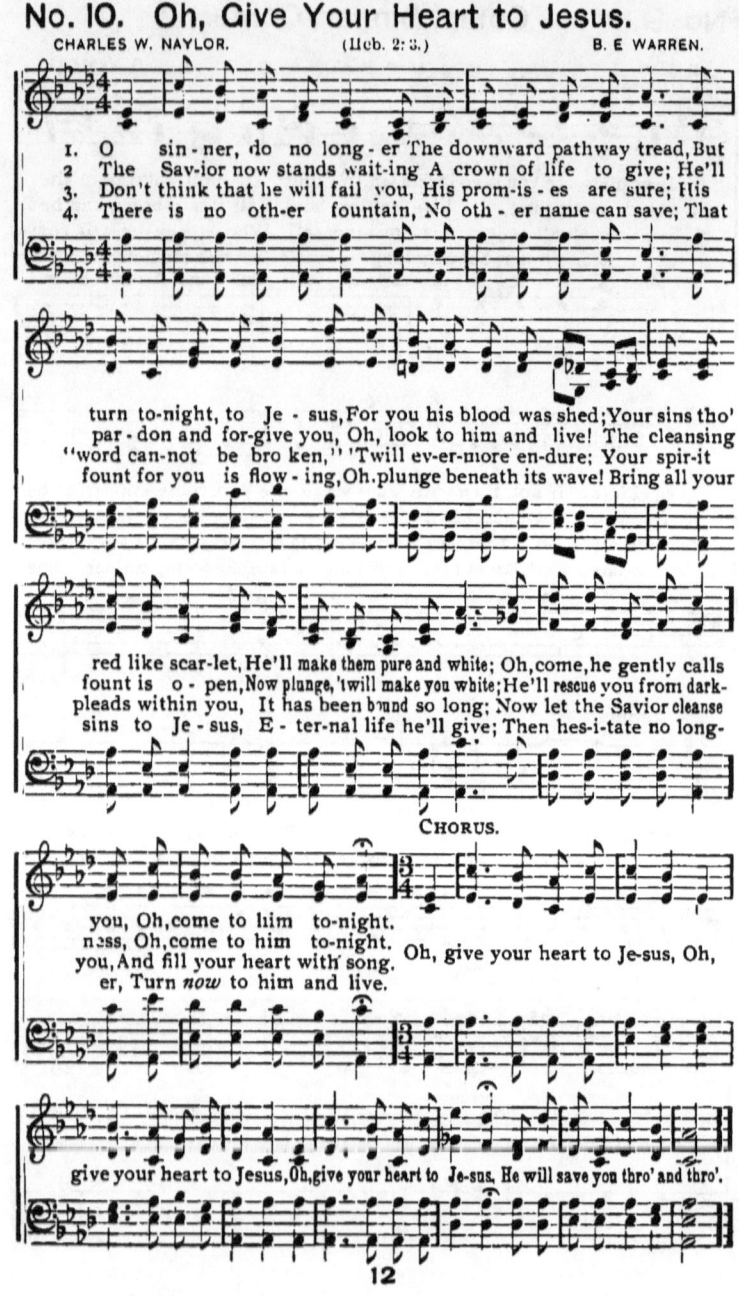

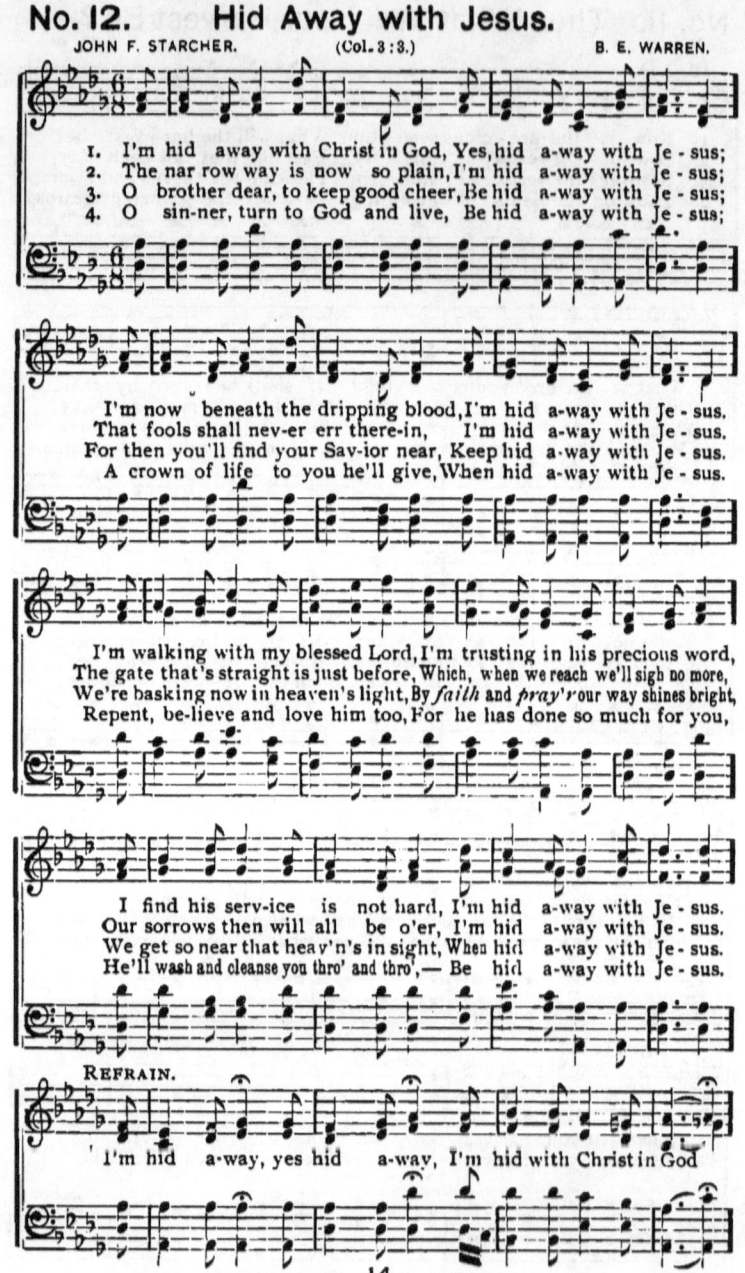

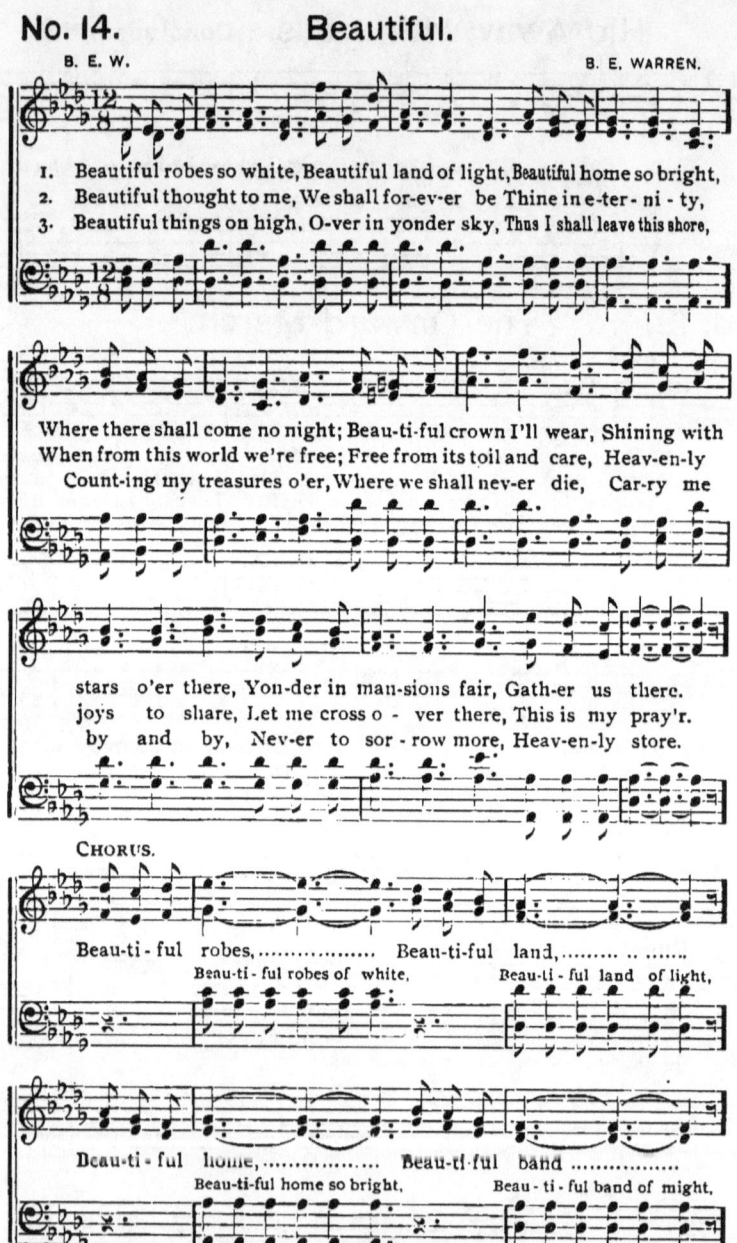

Beautiful. Concluded.

Beau-ti-ful crown,............ Shining so fair,............
Beau-ti-ful, beau-ti-ful crown, Shining, yes, shining so fair,

Beau-ti-ful man - sion bright, gather us there............
Beautiful mansion bright, gather us there, yes, gather us there.

No. 15. Complete in Christ.

S. L. S. (Col. 2:10.) S. L. SPECK. Har. for this work.

1. In Je - sus Christ I am complete, My soul is cleansed from sin;
2. In Je - sus Christ I am complete, My sins are all for - giv'n;
3. In Je - sus Christ I am complete, My needs are all sup - plied;
4. I'm in the liv-ing Church of God, In Christ I am com-plete;

His love in me is ev - er sweet, His grace a - bounds with - in.
To do his will, it is my meat, My name's enrolled in heav'n.
In him I have a safe re-treat, My soul is sanc - ti - fied.
Sup - port - ed by his precious word, I'll wor-ship at his feet.

D. S.—*Redeemed, redeemed just now complete, His love I will pro-claim.*

CHORUS. D. S.

Complete, complete, I'm all complete, Oh, glo - ry to his name!

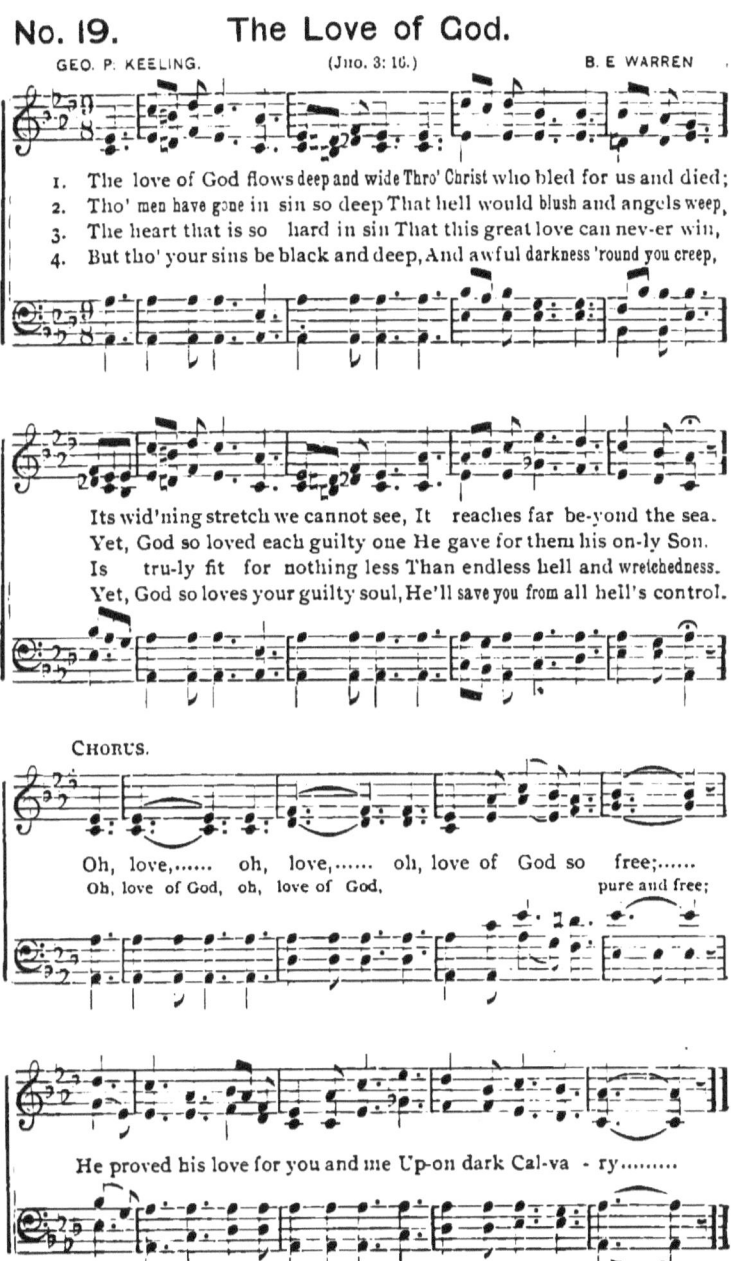

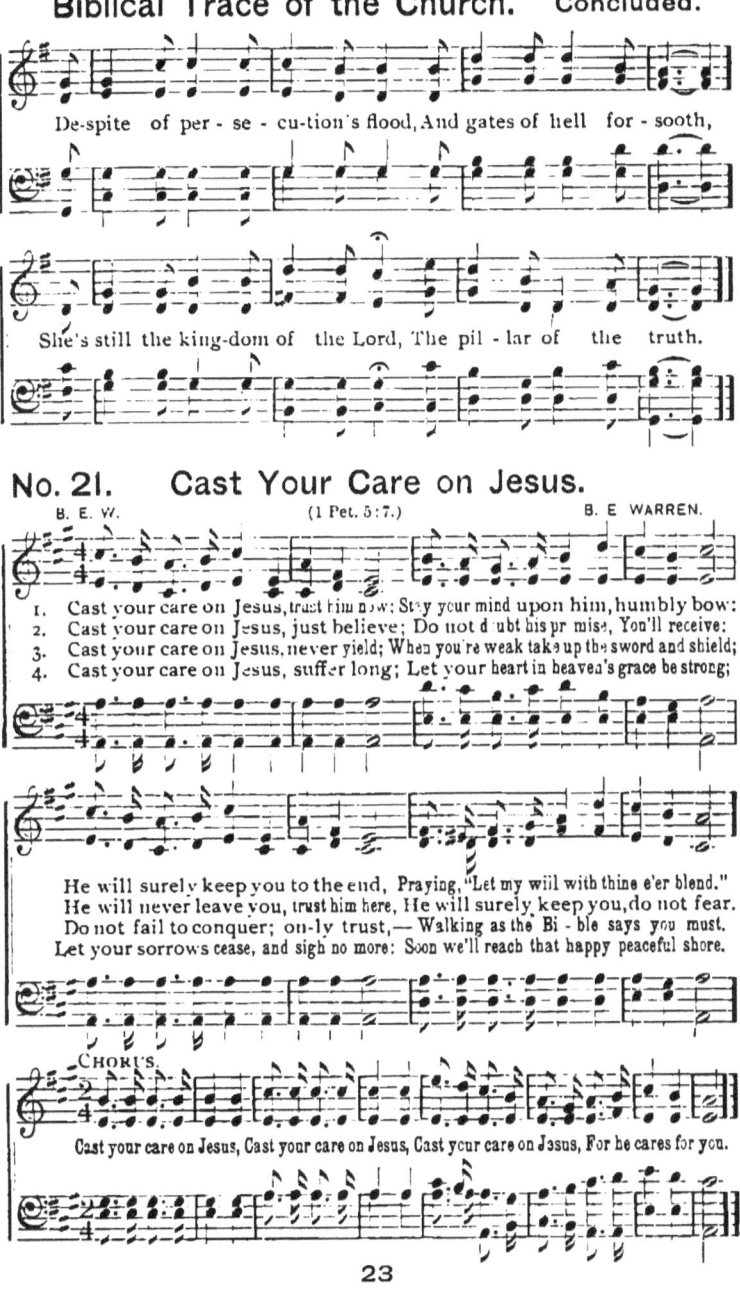

Our Needs Supplied. Concluded.

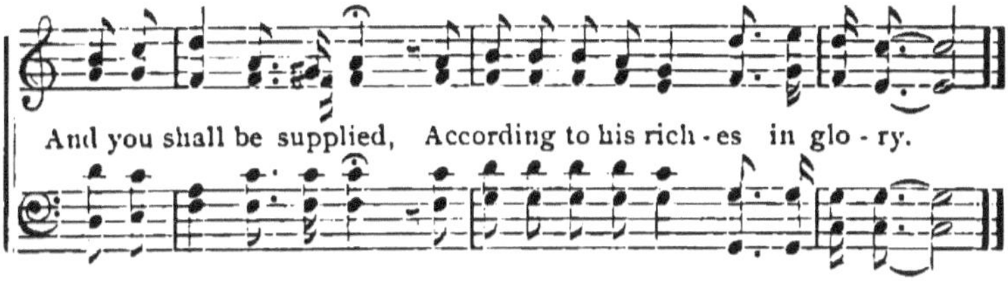

And you shall be supplied, According to his rich-es in glo-ry.

No. 25. He is Waiting.
Words and Melody by W. J. HENRY.   Har. for this work.

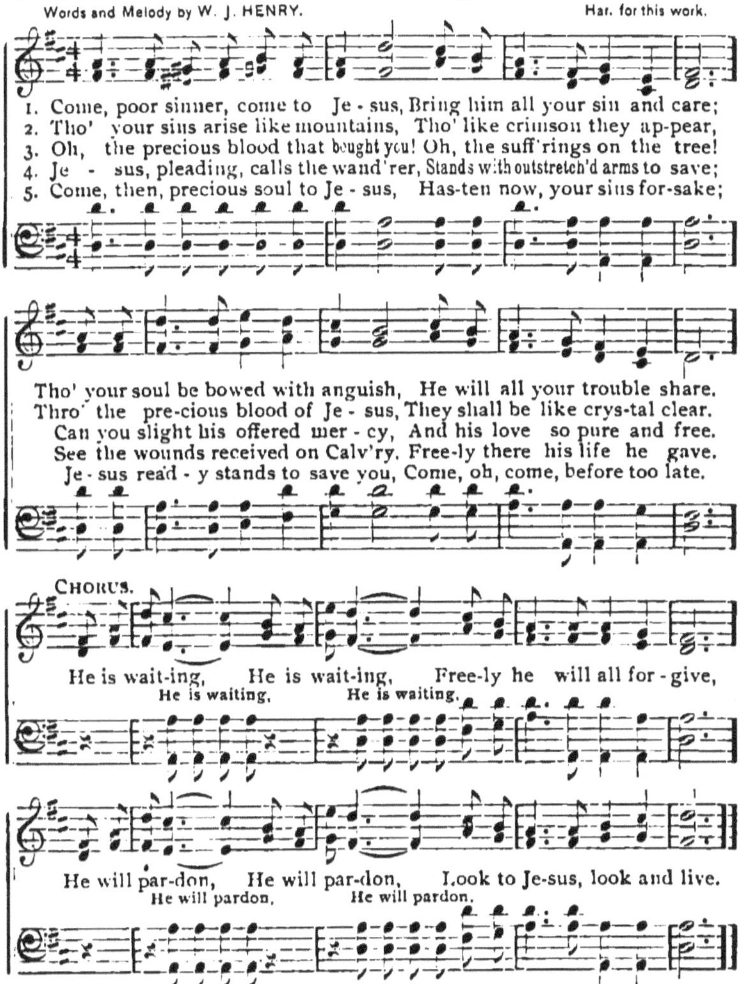

1. Come, poor sinner, come to Je-sus, Bring him all your sin and care;
2. Tho' your sins arise like mountains, Tho' like crimson they ap-pear,
3. Oh, the precious blood that bought you! Oh, the suff'rings on the tree!
4. Je-sus, pleading, calls the wand'rer, Stands with outstretch'd arms to save;
5. Come, then, precious soul to Je-sus, Has-ten now, your sins for-sake;

Tho' your soul be bowed with anguish, He will all your trouble share.
Thro' the pre-cious blood of Je-sus, They shall be like crys-tal clear.
Can you slight his offered mer-cy, And his love so pure and free.
See the wounds received on Calv'ry. Free-ly there his life he gave.
Je-sus read-y stands to save you, Come, oh, come, before too late.

CHORUS.

He is wait-ing, He is wait-ing, Free-ly he will all for-give,
He is waiting, He is waiting,

He will par-don, He will par-don, Look to Je-sus, look and live.
He will pardon, He will pardon.

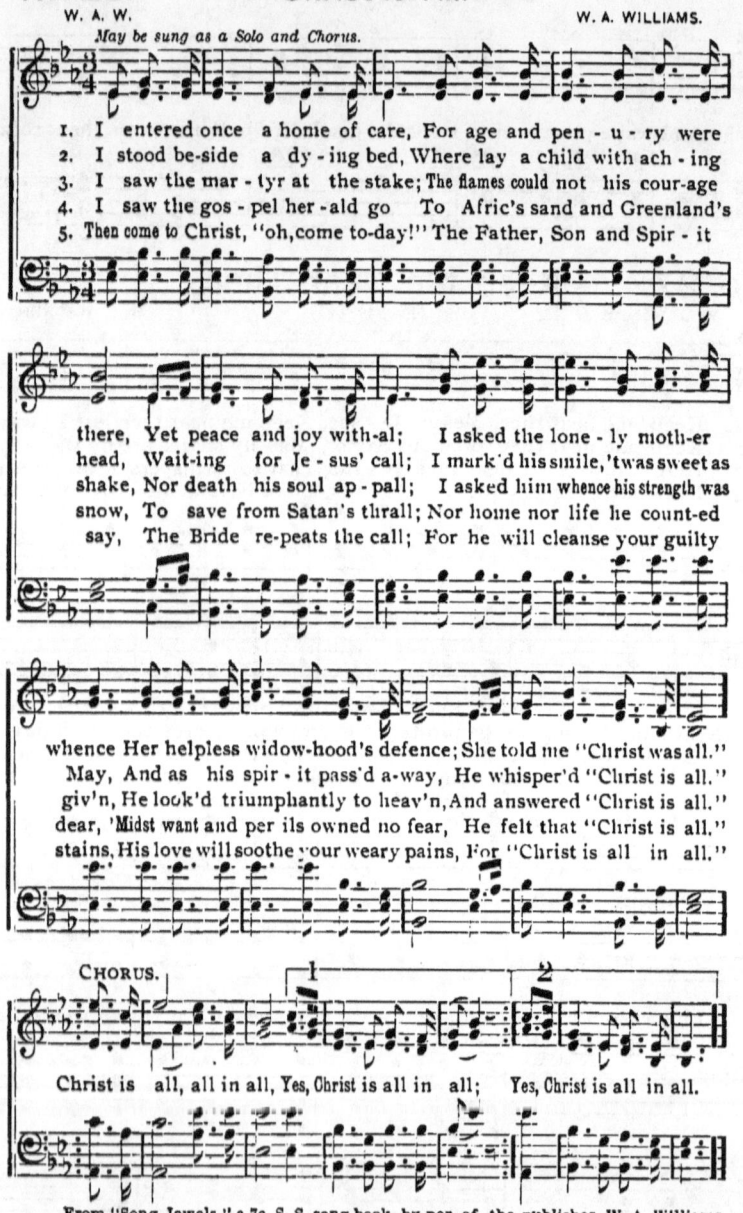

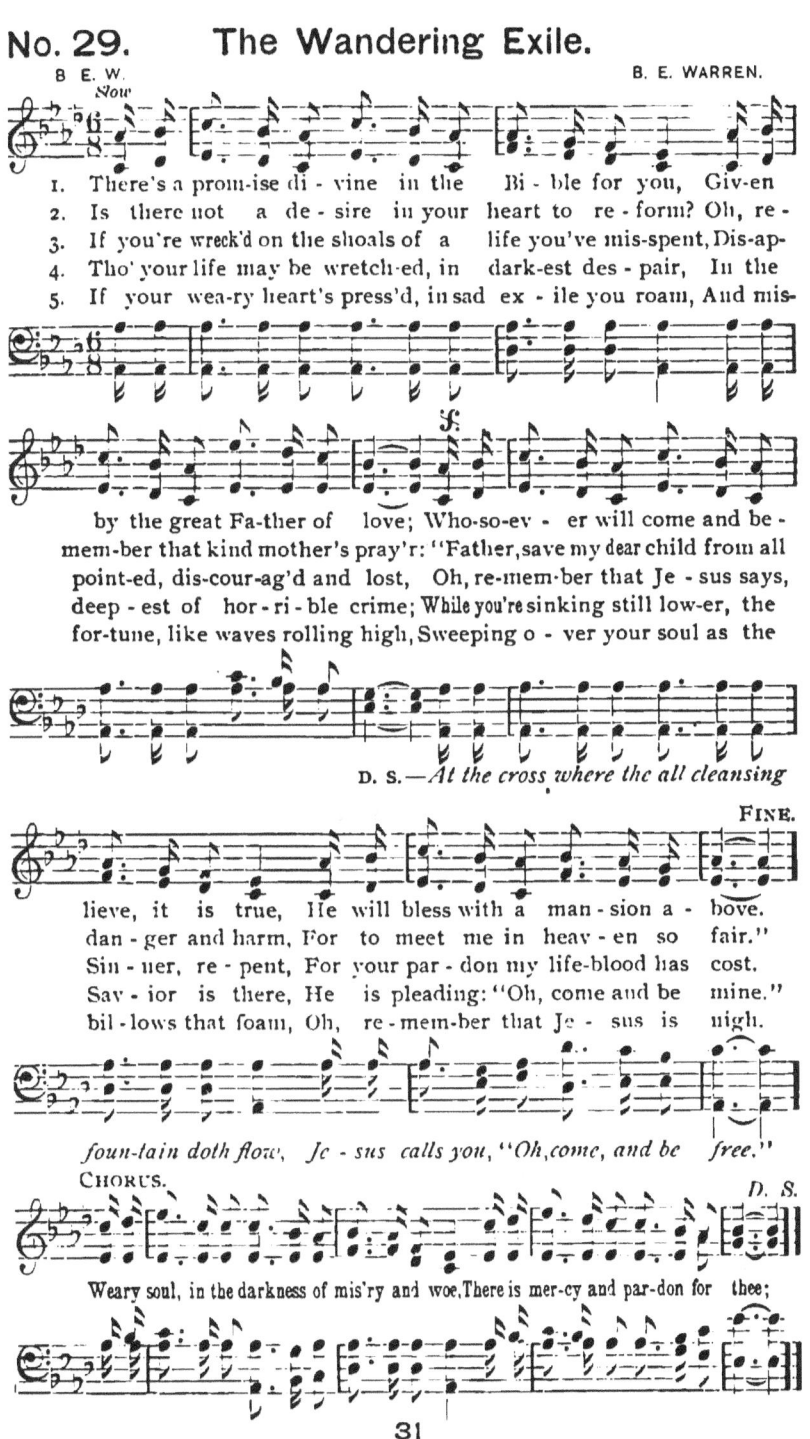

No. 31. Jesus, Thy Blood and Name.

F. L. HAHN. F. L. H. Harmonized by C. O. HINCKLEY.

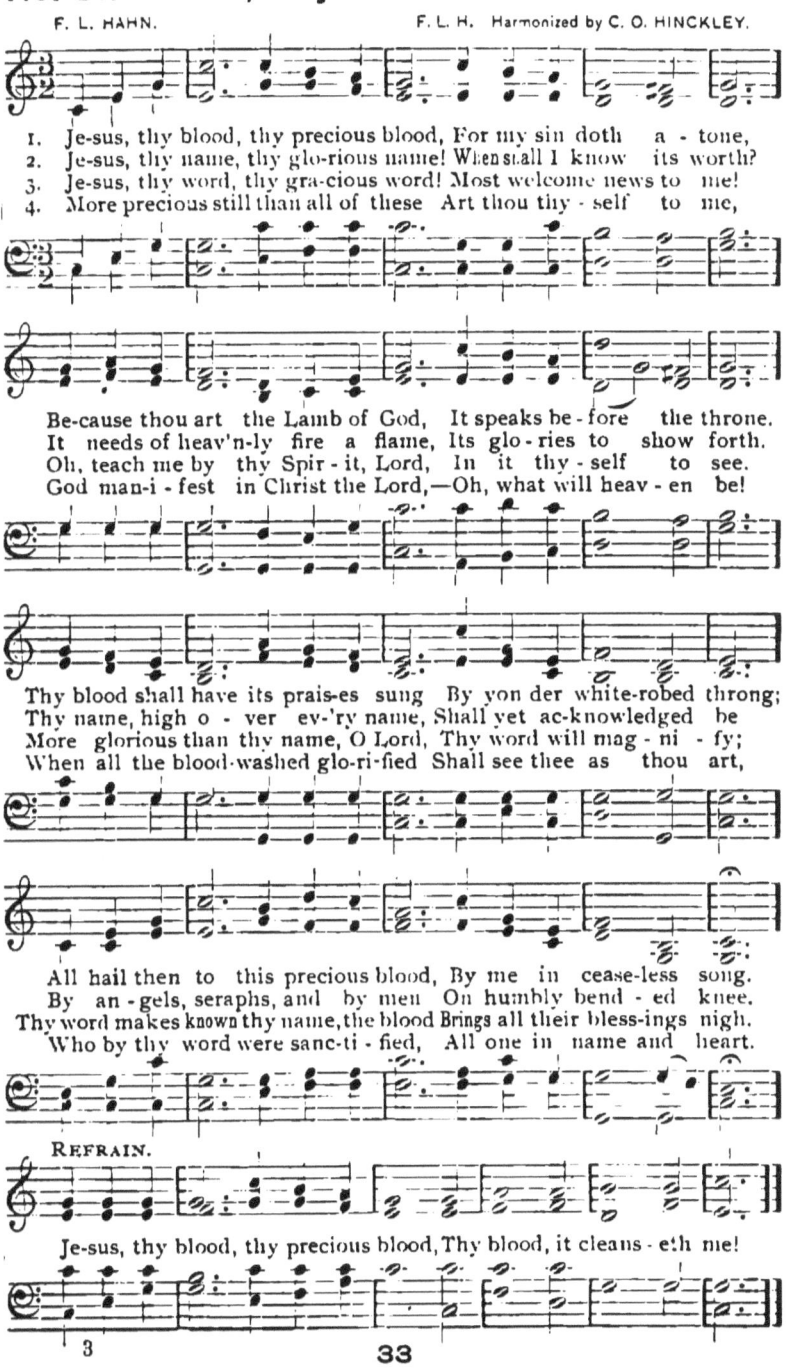

1. Je-sus, thy blood, thy precious blood, For my sin doth a-tone,
2. Je-sus, thy name, thy glo-rious name! When shall I know its worth?
3. Je-sus, thy word, thy gra-cious word! Most welcome news to me!
4. More precious still than all of these Art thou thy-self to me,

Be-cause thou art the Lamb of God, It speaks be-fore the throne.
It needs of heav'n-ly fire a flame, Its glo-ries to show forth.
Oh, teach me by thy Spir-it, Lord, In it thy-self to see.
God man-i-fest in Christ the Lord,—Oh, what will heav-en be!

Thy blood shall have its prais-es sung By yon der white-robed throng;
Thy name, high o-ver ev-'ry name, Shall yet ac-knowledged be
More glorious than thy name, O Lord, Thy word will mag-ni-fy;
When all the blood-washed glo-ri-fied Shall see thee as thou art,

All hail then to this precious blood, By me in cease-less song.
By an-gels, seraphs, and by men On humbly bend-ed knee.
Thy word makes known thy name, the blood Brings all their bless-ings nigh.
Who by thy word were sanc-ti-fied, All one in name and heart.

REFRAIN.

Je-sus, thy blood, thy precious blood, Thy blood, it cleans-eth me!

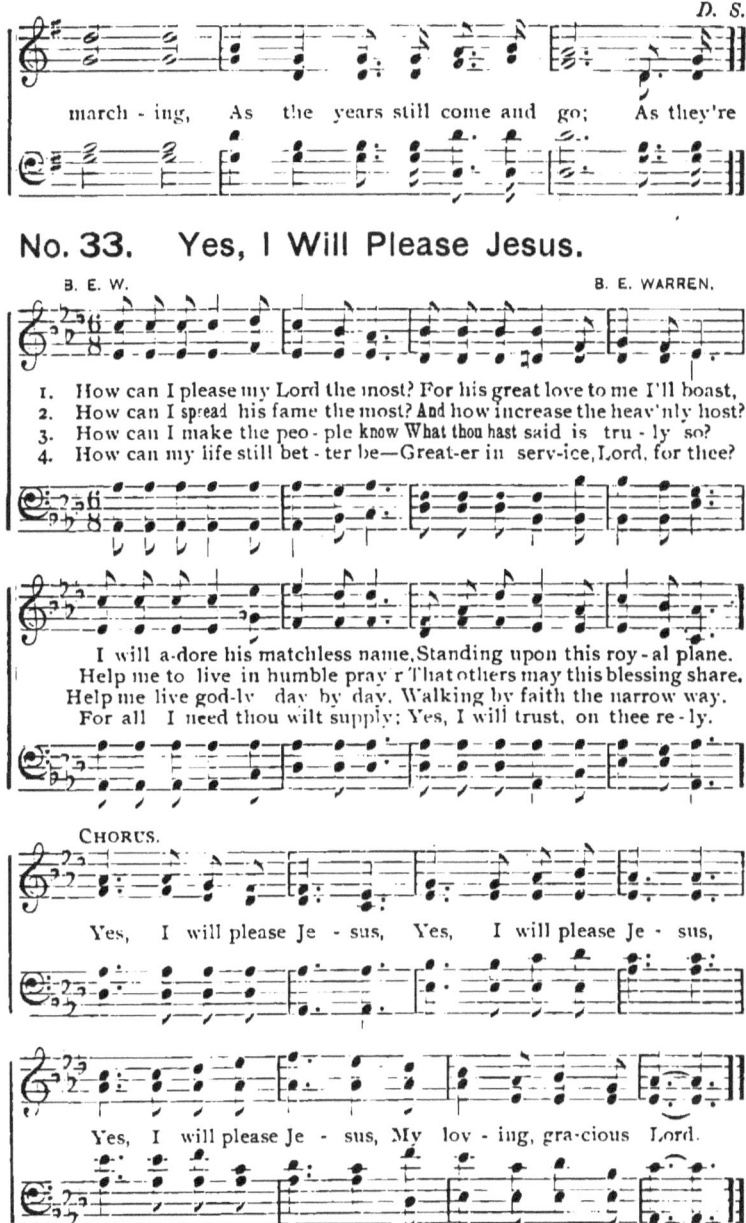

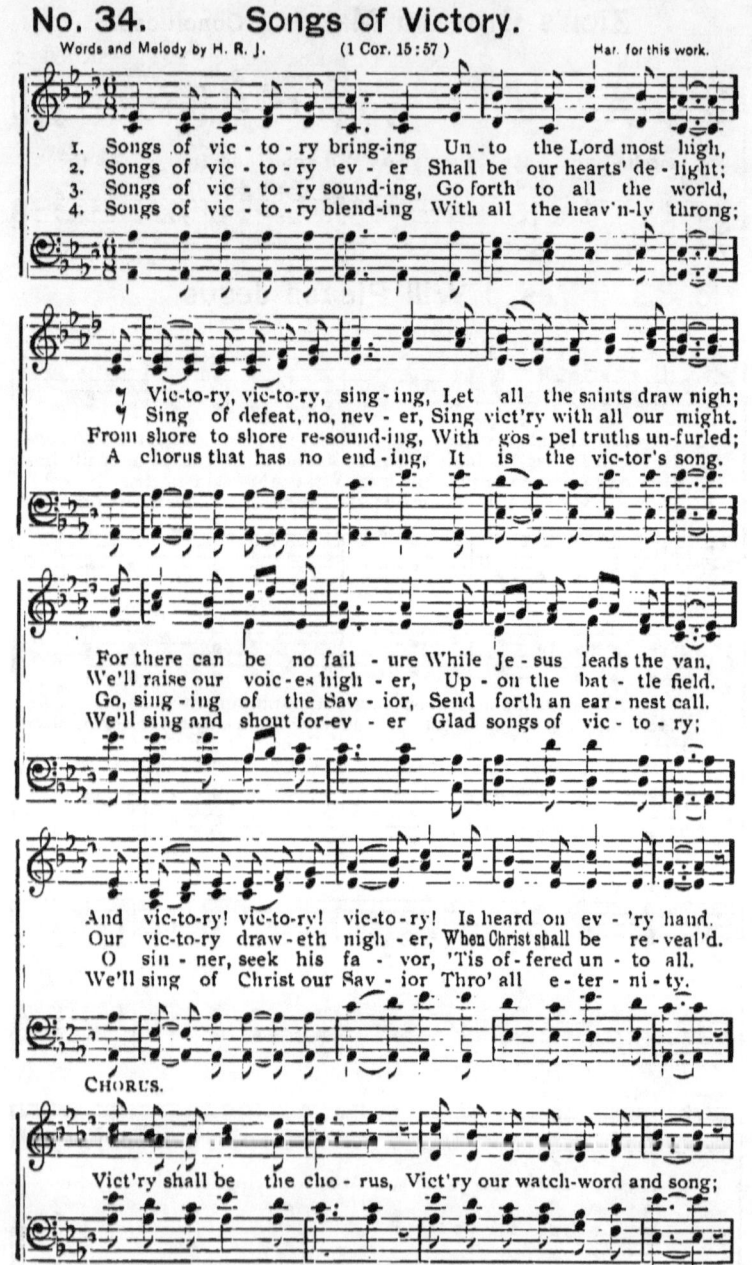

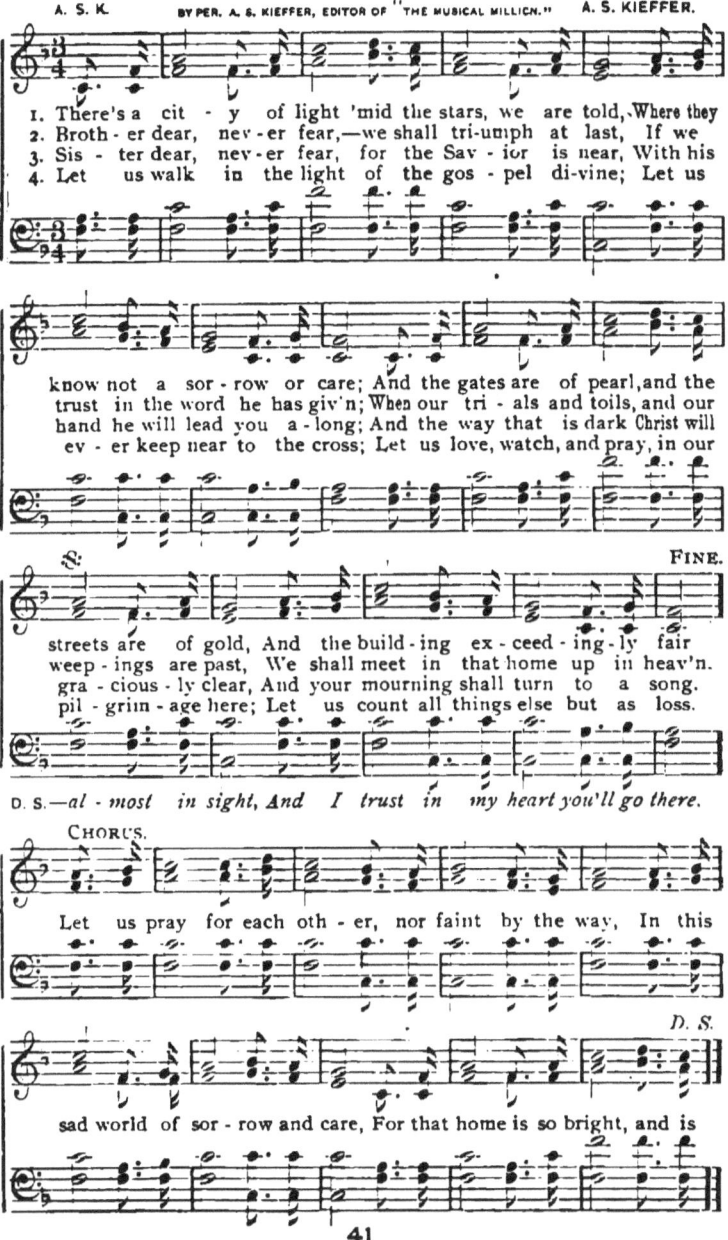

No. 41. The All-Cleansing Fountain.

FISHER. (Zech. 13:1.) Har. for this work.

1. There's a foun-tain o-pened in the house of God, Where the
2. When that fount was o-pened in the Sav-ior's side, How the
3. "Will you come and reason," saith the Lord,"with me, Tho' your
4. Yes, a bro-ken spir-it and a con-trite heart Thou wilt
5. I have o-ver-come now by the blood of the Lamb, And I'm
6. What are these in spot-less robes and whence came they, As they're

vil-est of sinners may go, And all test the pow-er of the
thief did re-joice in that day! And when dy-ing,"Lord re-mem-ber
sins red like crim-son do glow, And if dyed with scarlet stains your
nev-er des-pise, O my God! But wilt ful-ly cleanse it now in
clothed in my raiment so white; And I'm on my jour-ney to that
sing-ing with palms in their hands? These thro' trib-u-la-tion gain'd the

FINE. CHORUS.

crimson flood, Of the blood that makes whiter than snow.
me," he cried, Oh, the blood wash'd his sins all a way. Praise the Lord, I am
heart may be, I will make it as white as the snow."
ev'ry part, Till I'm whiter than snow by the blood.
glorious land, Where forever I'll dwell in the light. Praise the Lord,
victory, Having wash'd in the blood of the Lamb.

D. S.—*driven snow, I am wash'd in the blood of the Lamb.*

D. S.

washed In the all-cleansing blood of the Lamb, And my robes are whiter than the
I am wash'd of the Lamb,

No. 49. The Ninety-nine.

W. G. SCHELL. (Luke. 15:4-7.) B. E. WARREN.

Slow with expression.

1. The nine-ty-nine with-in the fold, Are safe from fears and storms of night,
2. The nine-ty-nine are safe to-day, They're all at home, so ful - ly blest,
3. The nine-ty-nine with care are fed, And rest within the shepherd's fold;
4. The shepherd dear aloud doth weep, Because one lamb a-far doth roam;

But one is on the mountains cold, 'Twill perish there—how sad the sight!
But one is wand'ring far a-way Up - on the mountain's snowy crest
But one is starv-ing, near-ly dead, Up'- on the mountains bare and cold.
The nine-ty-nine he'll safely keep,—We'll seek that lamb and bring it home.

CHORUS.

Go search it out, and bring it home, No more in darkness let it roam;

You'll find it there in dreadful plight, Oh! go and bring it back to-night.

I Hear My Savior Saying Etc. Concluded.

love has won my heart, And now we shall never, never, nev-er part.

No. 53.   Come, Prodigal Child.

B. E. WARREN.   J. B. VAUGHAN

1. Come, prodigal child, to your Fa-ther, Why feed on the mountains so bare?
2. Come, prodigal child, there is danger Of staying a-way too long;
3. Come, prodigal child, do not tar-ry; Why perish with hunger and cold?
4. Come, prodigal child, oh! remember From whence you are fallen, to roam;

I'm waiting, why stay any longer? There's bread enough and to spare.
Oh! stop where you are and remember You've gone from the right to the wrong.
Tho' fearful and wretched and weary, The Father says: "Come to the fold."
Make haste and return to the Father, Whose mercy will welcome you home.

CHORUS.

Come home,   come home,   Tho' wea-ry and tired you roam;
Come home, come home, come home, come home;

Come home,   come home,   O prod-i-gal child, come home.
Come home, come home, come home, come home,

Jesus Saves from Sin To-day. Concluded.

Jesus saves, yes, saves to-day, Jesus saves my soul to-day,
Jesus saves, saves to-day, Jesus saves my soul to-day,

No. 55. Endearing Lord.

BARNEY.   B. E. WARREN.

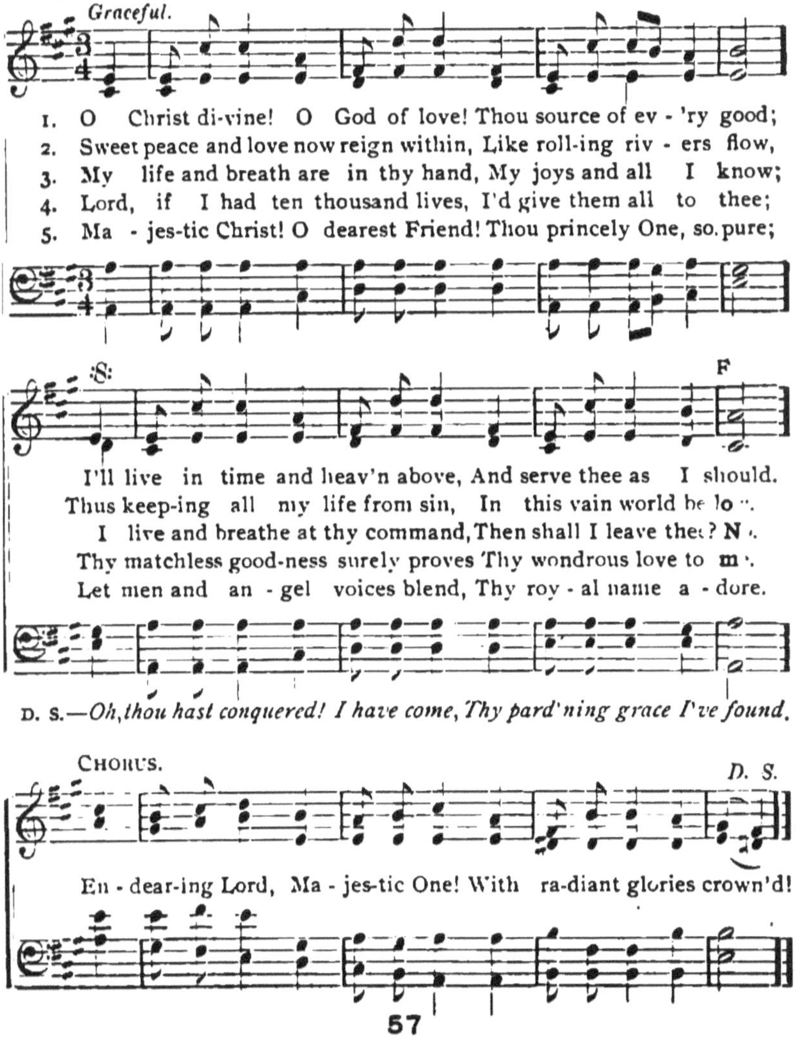

Graceful.

1. O Christ divine! O God of love! Thou source of ev-'ry good;
2. Sweet peace and love now reign within, Like roll-ing riv-ers flow,
3. My life and breath are in thy hand, My joys and all I know;
4. Lord, if I had ten thousand lives, I'd give them all to thee;
5. Ma-jes-tic Christ! O dearest Friend! Thou princely One, so pure;

I'll live in time and heav'n above, And serve thee as I should.
Thus keep-ing all my life from sin, In this vain world below.
I live and breathe at thy command, Then shall I leave thee? No.
Thy matchless good-ness surely proves Thy wondrous love to me.
Let men and an-gel voices blend, Thy roy-al name a-dore.

D. S.—*Oh, thou hast conquered! I have come, Thy pard'ning grace I've found.*

CHORUS.   D. S.

En-dear-ing Lord, Ma-jes-tic One! With ra-diant glories crown'd!

57

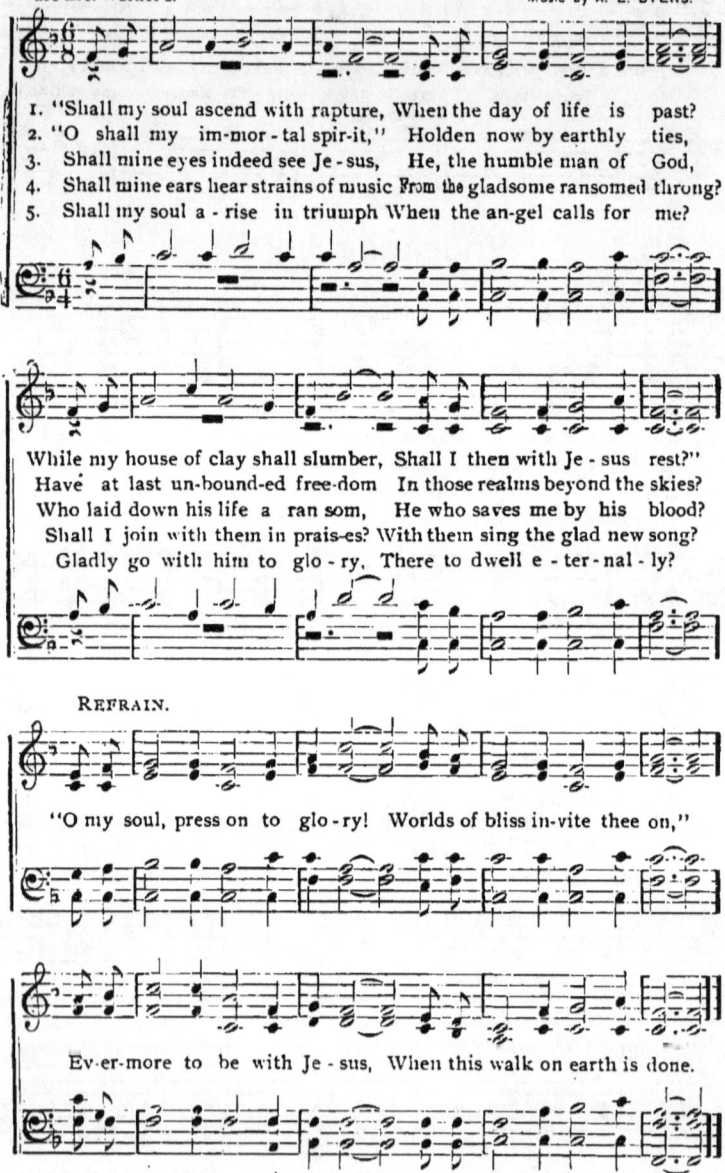

No. 56. The Last Hymn.

The following is a hymn begun by Bro. D. S. Warner shortly before his death, and recently completed by Sister Georgia Elliott. The words enclosed by quotation marks are Bro. Warner's.

Music by A. L. BYERS.

1. "Shall my soul ascend with rapture, When the day of life is past?
2. "O shall my im-mor-tal spir-it," Holden now by earthly ties,
3. Shall mine eyes indeed see Je-sus, He, the humble man of God,
4. Shall mine ears hear strains of music From the gladsome ransomed throng?
5. Shall my soul a-rise in triumph When the an-gel calls for me?

While my house of clay shall slumber, Shall I then with Je-sus rest?"
Have at last un-bound-ed free-dom In those realms beyond the skies?
Who laid down his life a ran som, He who saves me by his blood?
Shall I join with them in prais-es? With them sing the glad new song?
Gladly go with him to glo-ry, There to dwell e-ter-nal-ly?

REFRAIN.

"O my soul, press on to glo-ry! Worlds of bliss in-vite thee on,"

Ev-er-more to be with Je-sus, When this walk on earth is done.

No. 57.   The Golden Harvest.

H. R. J.   (John 4:35.)   H. R. JEFFREY.
                                       Har. by B. E. W.

1. Oh, why should I be i-dle, While there's so much to do?
2. Oh, why should I be i-dle? The morn-ing sun is high,
3. No, I shall not be i-dle, For in God's word I see:
4. I'll be no long-er i-dle, But faith-ful I will be;
5. Why stand ye all day i-dle? There's har-vest-ing for all;

The wheat is ripe to har-vest, And the la-bor-ers are few.
And soon it will be sink-ing Low in the west-ern sky.
"No i-dlers in my vine-yard; Go thou and work for me."
I'll go and work for Je-sus, I hear him call-ing me.
Oh, grasp the flam-ing sick-le, And heed the Mas-ter's call.

CHORUS.

The la-bor-ers are few,...... And still there's much to do;......
          too few,   to do;

The wheat is ripe to har-vest, And the la-bor-ers are few.

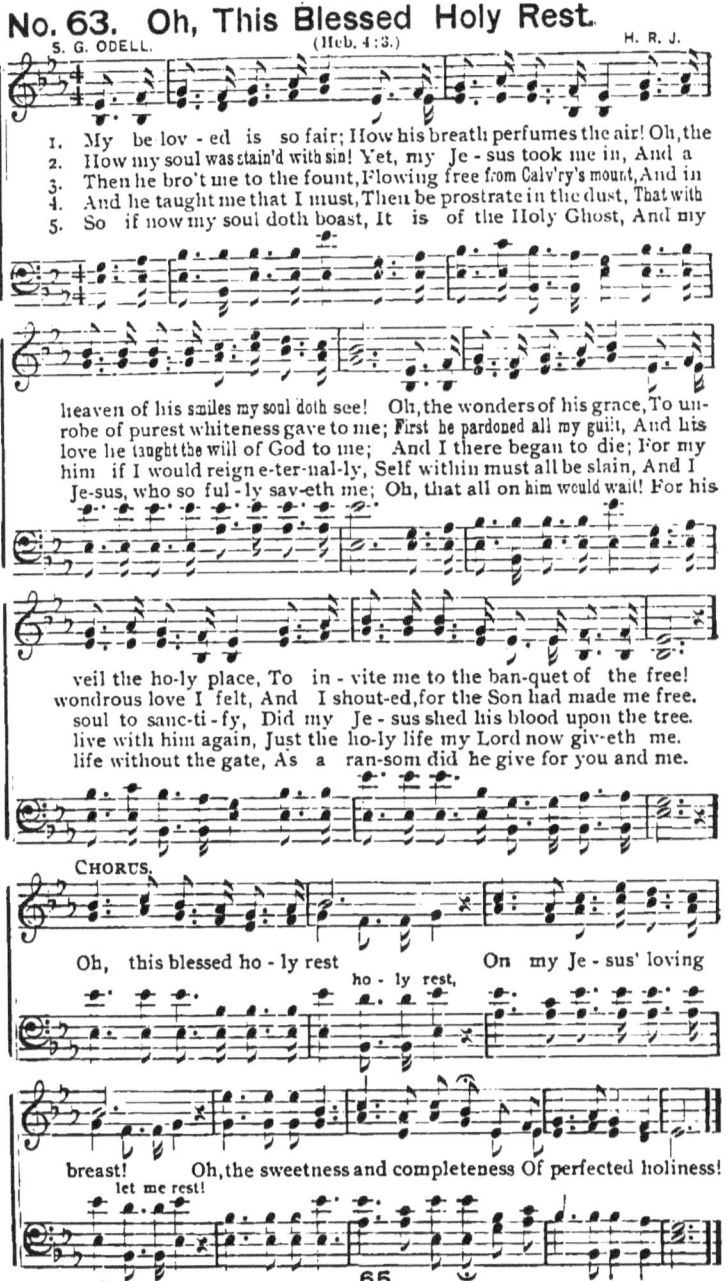

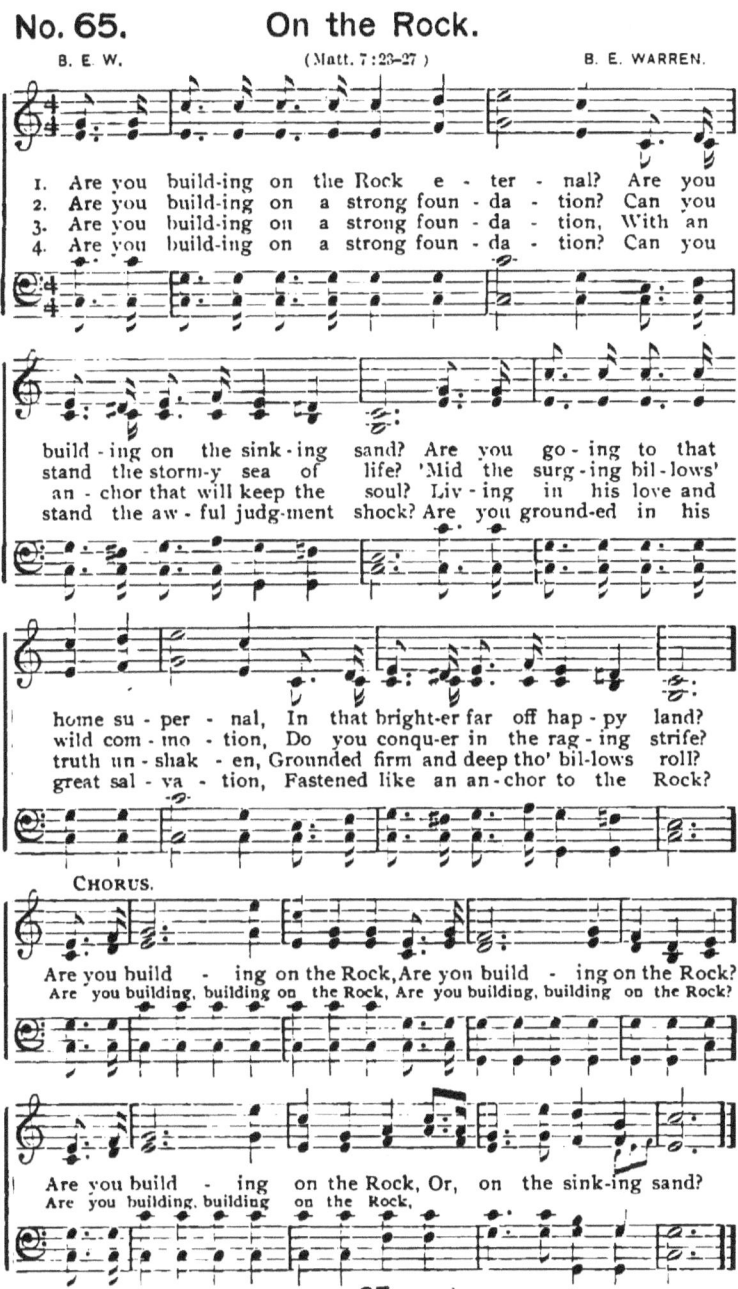

I Ought to Love My Savior. Concluded.

Love drew him down from heav-en To seek and save the lost.
That I should not be ban-ished, But in his glo-ry dwell.
"'Tis finished!"—my sal-va-tion, Thine shall the glo-ry be.
This world, oh, wondrous sto-ry, 'Tis love, re-deem-ing love.
And flood this earth-en tem-ple With glo-ry from thy throne.

No. 67. Humility.

WM. G. SCHELL. C. E. HUNTER.

1. Hu-mil-i-ty, thou se-cret vale, Un-known to proud in heart;
2. Hu-mil-i-ty, how pure thy place! Thou seat of ho-li-ness!
3. Hu-mil-i-ty, how calm the breast That knows thy peace sublime!
4. Hu-mil-i-ty, thou shore-less sea Of per-fect love so deep!

Where show'rs of bless-ing nev-er fail, And glo-ries ne'er de-part.
Thou door of en-trance in-to grace And ev-er-last-ing bliss!
With-in thy courts our per-fect rest Grows sweeter all the time.
Thy crys-tal wa-ters cov-er me, My help-less soul to keep.

CHORUS.

Oh, make thy blest a-bode with me, Thou an-gel of the sky;
If I may ev-er dwell with thee, My soul shall nev-er die.

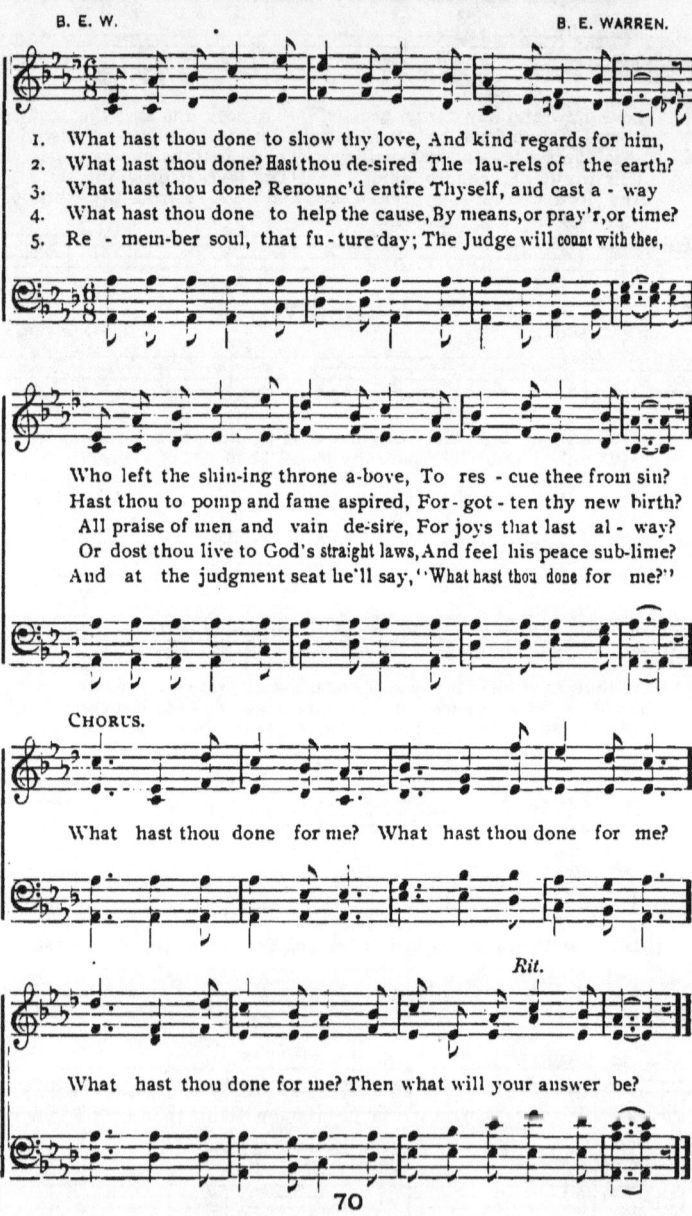

No. 71. Praise God for the Bible.

W. F. CRAFTS. Words arr.
TUNE:—*Home, Sweet Home.*

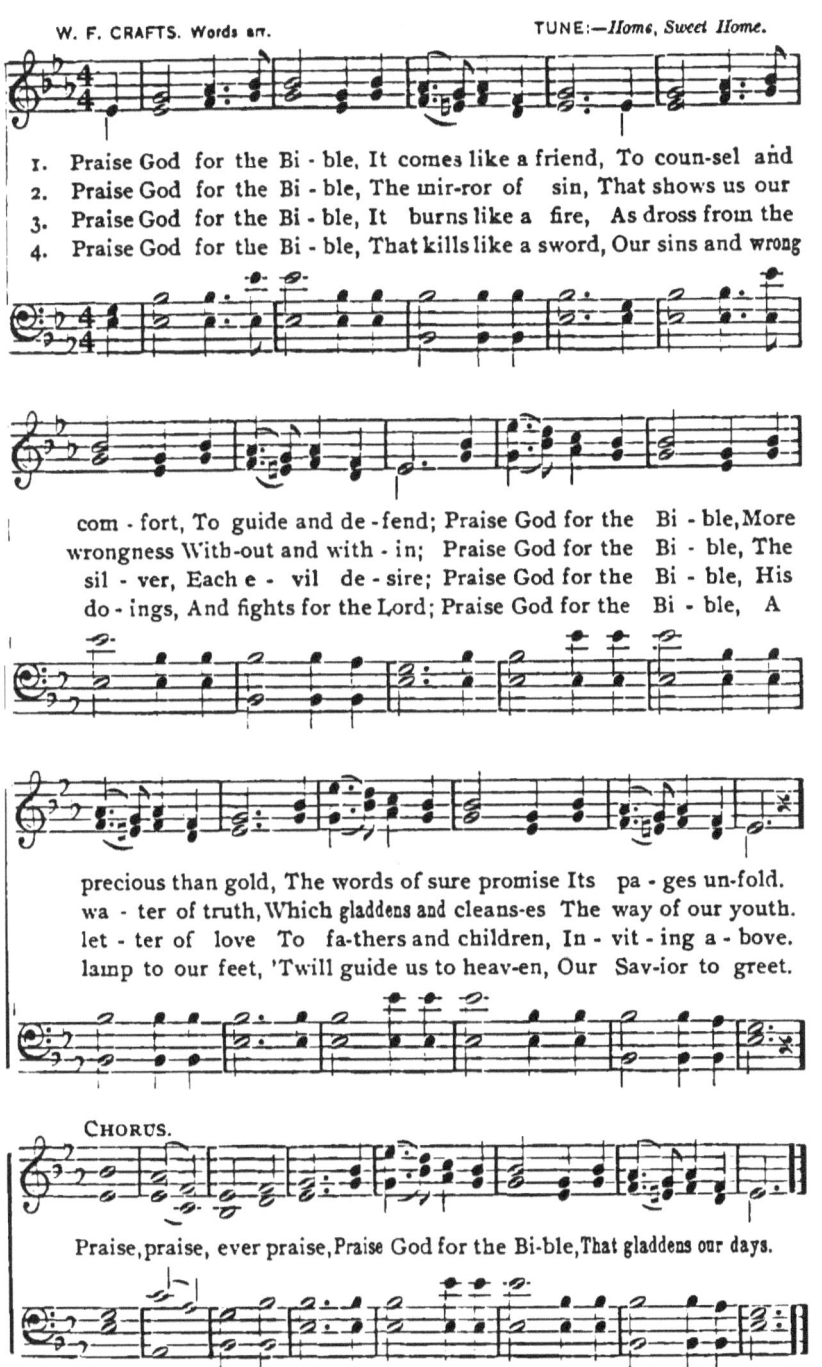

1. Praise God for the Bi - ble, It comes like a friend, To coun-sel and
2. Praise God for the Bi - ble, The mir-ror of sin, That shows us our
3. Praise God for the Bi - ble, It burns like a fire, As dross from the
4. Praise God for the Bi - ble, That kills like a sword, Our sins and wrong

com - fort, To guide and de - fend; Praise God for the Bi - ble, More
wrongness With-out and with - in; Praise God for the Bi - ble, The
sil - ver, Each e - vil de - sire; Praise God for the Bi - ble, His
do - ings, And fights for the Lord; Praise God for the Bi - ble, A

precious than gold, The words of sure promise Its pa - ges un-fold.
wa - ter of truth, Which gladdens and cleans-es The way of our youth.
let - ter of love To fa-thers and children, In - vit - ing a - bove.
lamp to our feet, 'Twill guide us to heav-en, Our Sav-ior to greet.

CHORUS.

Praise, praise, ever praise, Praise God for the Bi-ble, That gladdens our days.

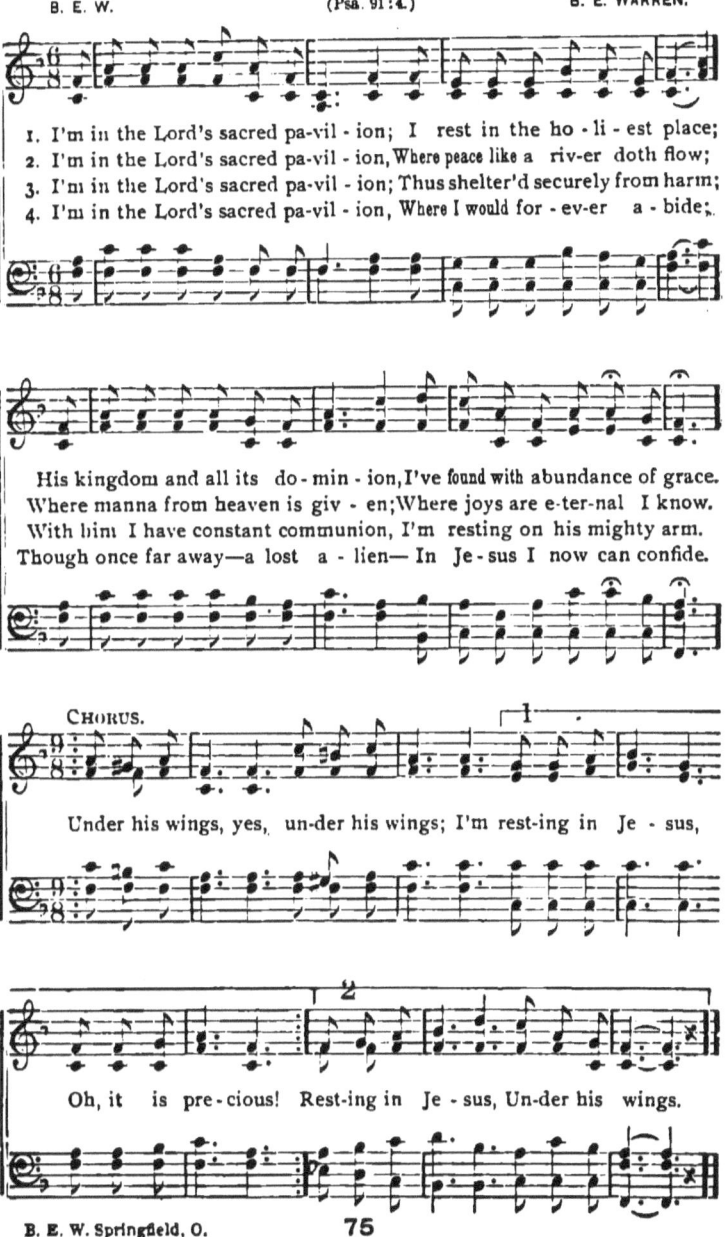

No. 74. To Be Lost in the Night.

A. F. FERRIS.   ELLA B. BISHOP.

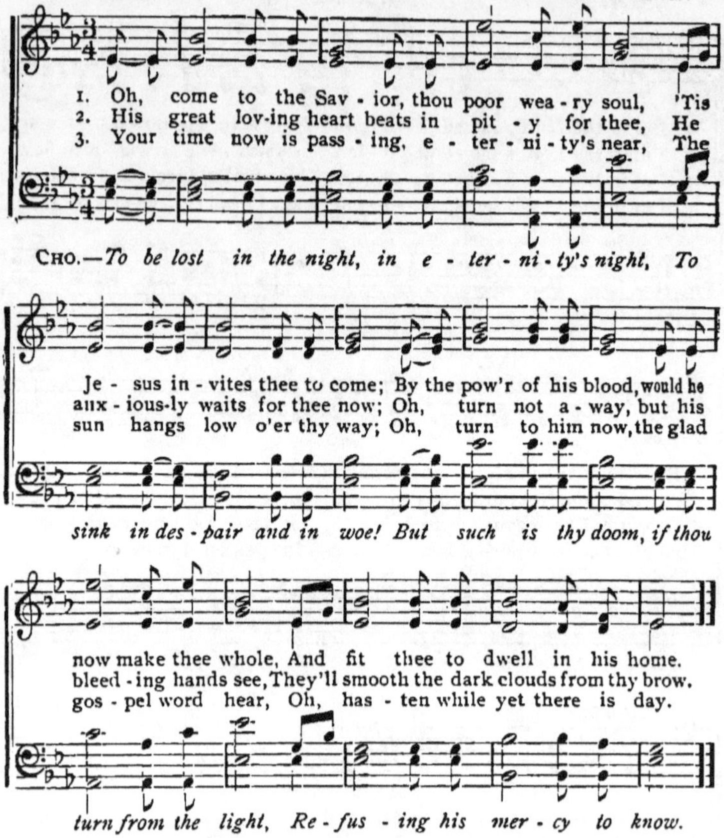

1. Oh, come to the Sav-ior, thou poor wea-ry soul, 'Tis
2. His great lov-ing heart beats in pit-y for thee, He
3. Your time now is pass-ing, e-ter-ni-ty's near, The

CHO.—To be lost in the night, in e-ter-ni-ty's night, To

Je - sus in-vites thee to come; By the pow'r of his blood, would he
anx - ious-ly waits for thee now; Oh, turn not a-way, but his
sun hangs low o'er thy way; Oh, turn to him now, the glad

sink in des-pair and in woe! But such is thy doom, if thou

now make thee whole, And fit thee to dwell in his home.
bleed - ing hands see, They'll smooth the dark clouds from thy brow.
gos - pel word hear, Oh, has-ten while yet there is day.

turn from the light, Re - fus - ing his mer - cy to know.

From "Songs of the Reapers," by per.

No. 75. Precious Home of Rest.

B E W.   B. E. WARREN.

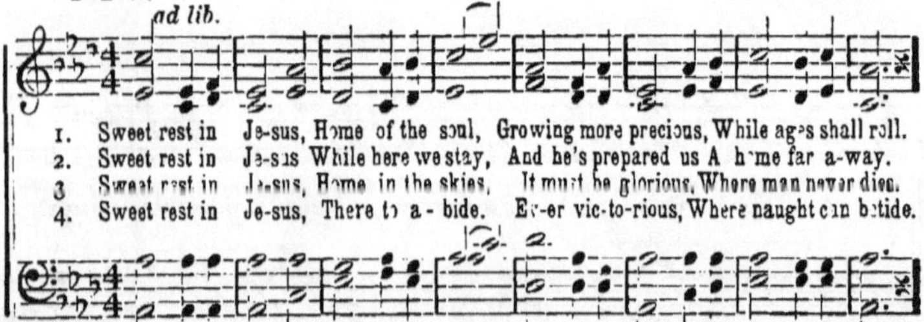

ad lib.

1. Sweet rest in Je-sus, Home of the soul, Growing more precious, While ages shall roll.
2. Sweet rest in Je-sus While here we stay, And he's prepared us A home far a-way.
3. Sweet rest in Je-sus, Home in the skies, It must be glorious, Where man never dies.
4. Sweet rest in Je-sus, There to a-bide. Ev-er vic-to-rious, Where naught can betide.

No. 78. Sinner, Christ is Waiting.

JOSEPH.   J. C. F.

1. Come, poor sin-ner, Christ is waiting, For to soothe thy heart of pain;
2. Come to him, why will you languish, Filled with sor - row and de - spair?
3. Calm-ly then, with sweet e - mo-tion, Thy poor soul shall sink to rest
4. Quickly catch the beams of glo-ry, Streaming forth from Calv'ry's cross.
5. Do not doubt nor wait a mo-ment, Soon the cleansing will be done;

He is anx - ious, he is will-ing, Come, he'll cleanse you from each stain.
All the clouds will quickly van-ish, Leav-ing all like morning fair.
In the depth of love's pure ocean, Where you'll be for - ev - er blest.
Where his blood was shed to save you, Oh, how much thy soul has cost!
Then he'll clothe thee in white raiment, That will far out - shine the sun.

CHORUS.

Come, oh, come then, do not tar - ry, He will fill thy heart with joy;

Hasten quick - ly, he will cleanse thee, Pure as gold with-out al - loy.

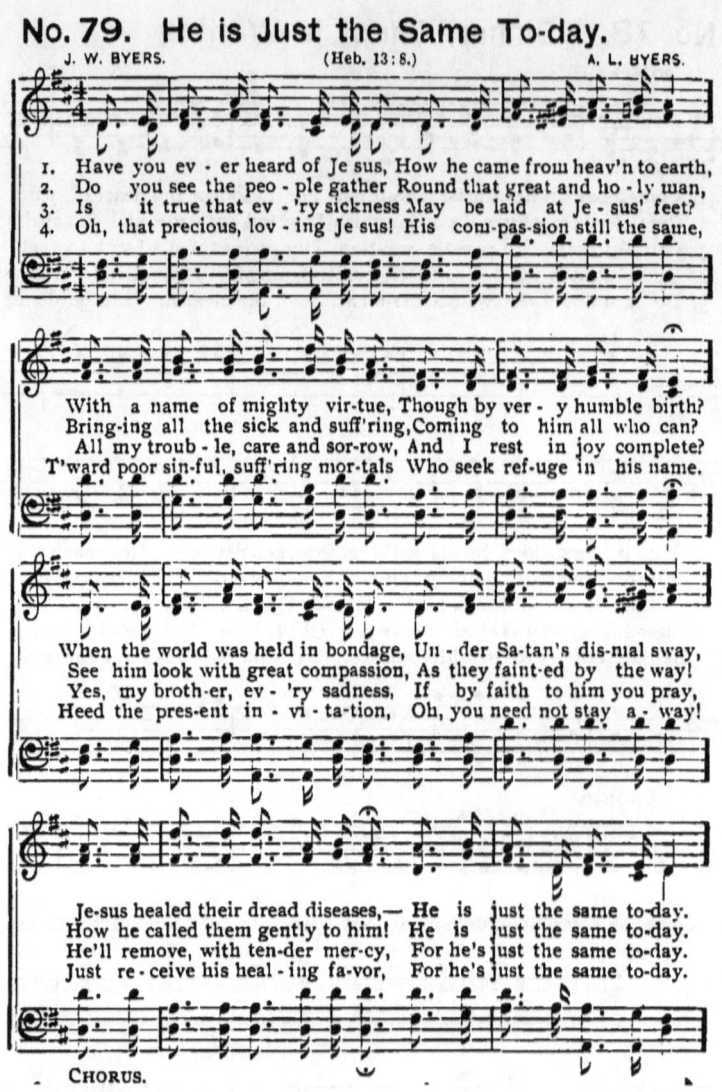

To the Cross. Concluded.

D. S.

don't de-lay, Live or die, in its glo-ry we will here forever stay,
don't de-lay,

No. 84. I Am from Sin Set Free.

(Rom. 6:22.) Chorus and Music by H. R. JEFFREY.

1. Let worldly minds the world pursue, It has no charms for me;
2. Its pleasures can no longer please, Nor hap - pi - ness af - ford;
3. As by the light of opening day The stars are all concealed,
4. Creatures no more di - vide my choice, I bid them all de - part;

FINE.

Once I ad-mired its tri - fles too, But grace hath set me free.
Far from my heart be joys like these, Now I have seen the Lord.
So earth-ly pleasures fade a-way, When Je - sus is re - vealed.
His name, his love, his gracious voice, Have fixed my rov-ing heart.

D. S —*This world has now no charms for me, For Christ hath set me free.*

CHORUS. *D. S.*

Free! free! free! I am from sin set free!

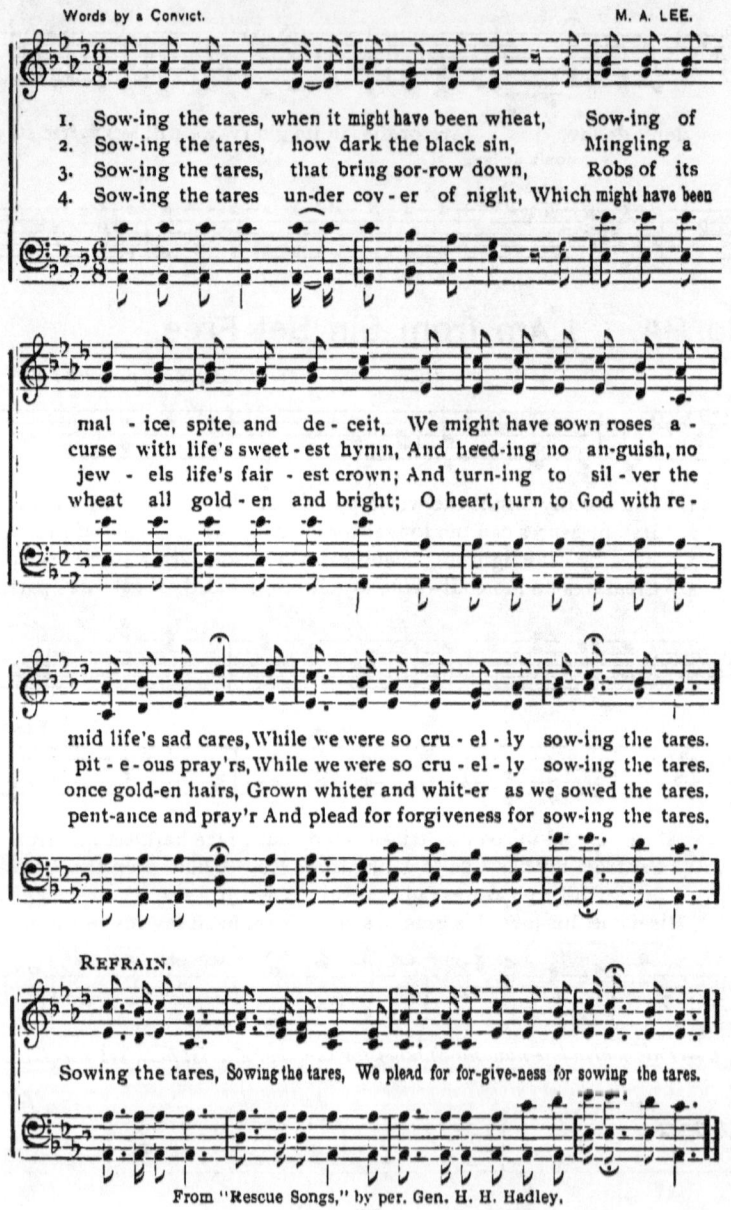

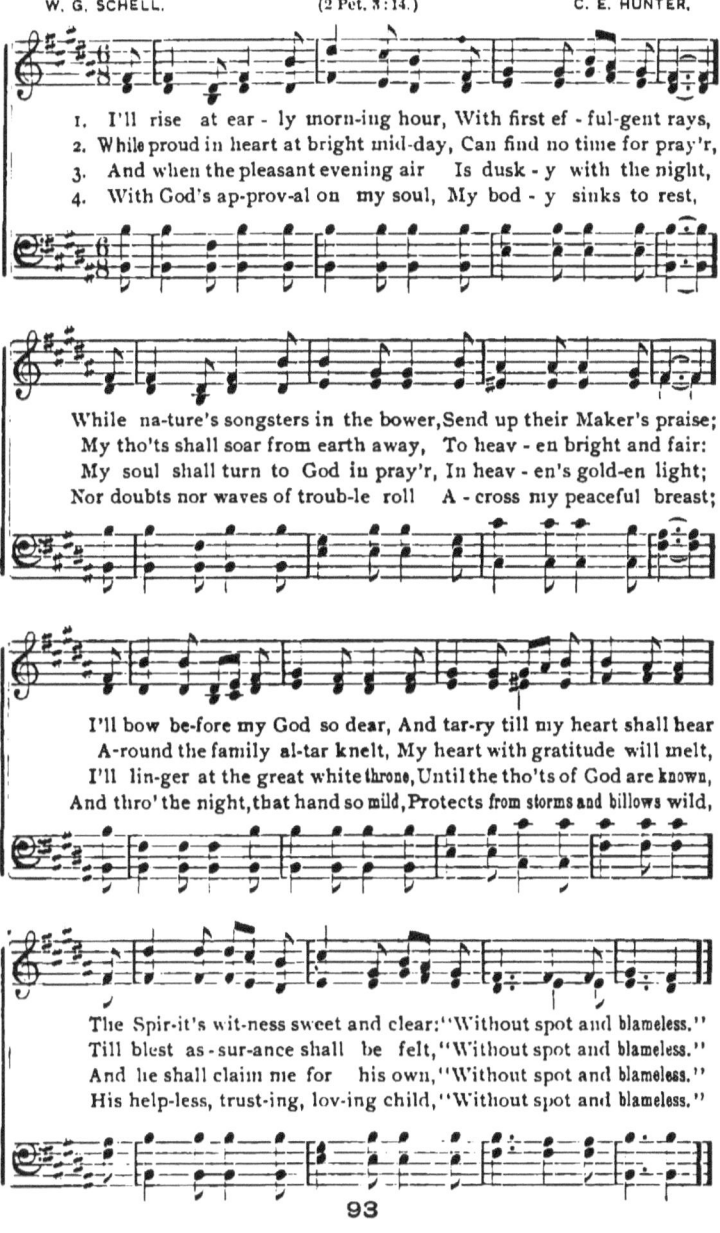

No. 96. Rays of Hope.

D. S. WARNER. (Col. 1:27.) W. J. C. THIEL.

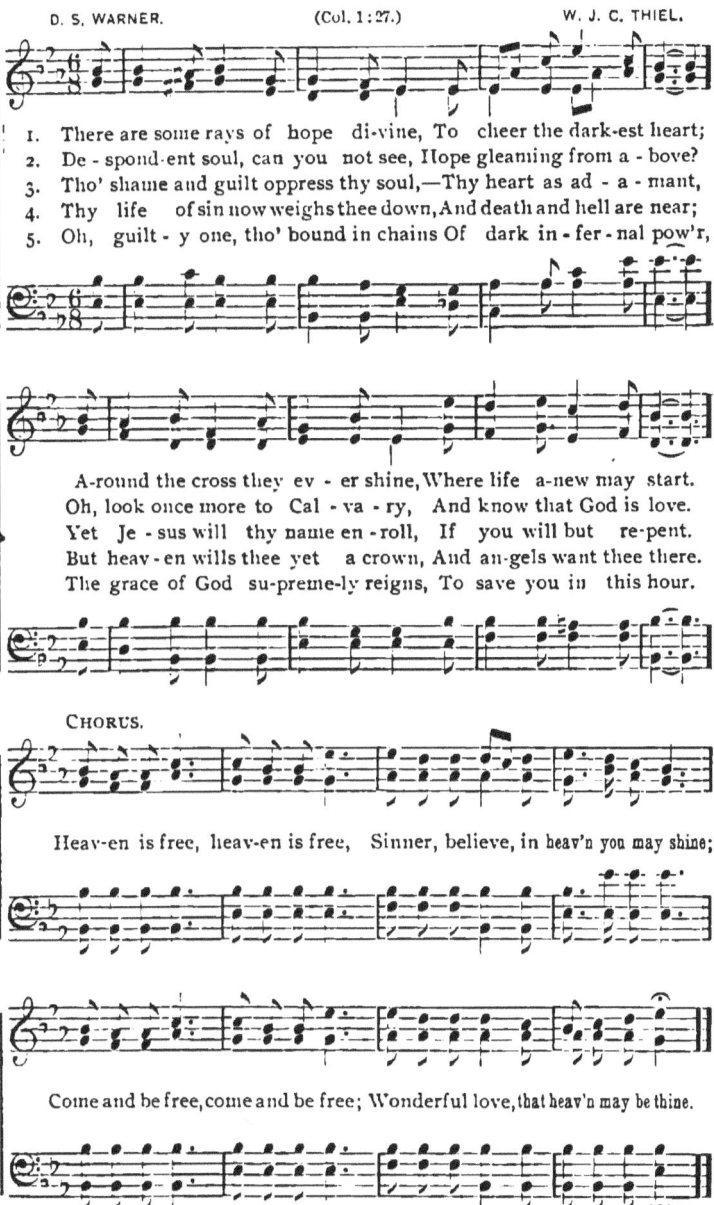

1. There are some rays of hope di-vine, To cheer the dark-est heart;
2. De-spond-ent soul, can you not see, Hope gleaming from a-bove?
3. Tho' shame and guilt oppress thy soul,—Thy heart as ad-a-mant,
4. Thy life of sin now weighs thee down, And death and hell are near;
5. Oh, guilt-y one, tho' bound in chains Of dark in-fer-nal pow'r,

A-round the cross they ev-er shine, Where life a-new may start.
Oh, look once more to Cal-va-ry, And know that God is love.
Yet Je-sus will thy name en-roll, If you will but re-pent.
But heav-en wills thee yet a crown, And an-gels want thee there.
The grace of God su-preme-ly reigns, To save you in this hour.

CHORUS.

Heav-en is free, heav-en is free, Sinner, believe, in heav'n you may shine;

Come and be free, come and be free; Wonderful love, that heav'n may be thine.

No. 98. A Prayer in Song.

W. M. WOLCOTT. Melody by Mrs. A. J. SHRIVER.

1. Sav-ior, thou art life to me, Guard me by thy watchful eye;
2. Help me, Lord, to faithful be, Give me grace to do thy will,
3. Teach me from thy blessed word, Les-sons precious to my soul;
4. Oh, thou art my ref-uge here, All my hopes are built on thee;

Ev - er by thy Spir-it be Thou a guide to worlds on high.
That thro' all e-ter-ni-ty, Ho-ly love my soul may thrill.
Help me un-der stand it, Lord, By it make and keep me whole.
From all sin and slavish fear, Je-sus makes me ful-ly free.

Hide me from the storms of life; Keep me from the tempter's snare;
For tho' blest by world-ly store, Sanctioned by the creeds of men,
By thy word we stand or fall, By thy word we live or did;
So when all my toils are o'er, Let me gain that blest a-bode,

And while here 'mid toil and strife, Let me cast on thee my care.
Je-sus says, "I am the door,"—He alone can save from sin.
If by part and not by all, Then we make thy word a lie.
And with loved ones gone before, Ev - er dwell with thee, my God.

No. 99. Near the End.

W. G. SCHELL. (Rev. 10:5-7.) A. L. BYERS.

1. Time moves on with solemn footsteps, As it nears the fi-nal shore;
2. Lo! the an-gel now is standing On the sea and on the land;
3. One more trum-pet yet to summon Us be-fore the judgment seat,
4. While false prophets are con-fid-ing In a fool-ish err-ing dream

Fast the sun of earth is sink-ing, Soon our world shall be no more.
How his voice the air is rending, As to God he lifts his hand!
Then the time of our frail plan-et Will be said to be com-plete.
Of mil-len - ni - al enjoyments, They neglect the cleansing stream.

The sixth trumpet now is sounding, To prepare the ho - ly bride;—
What an aw-ful, aw-ful mes-sage! Help us, Lord, this truth to see:
How the wick-ed will be wail-ing, And the righteous o - ver-joyed,
O poor sinner, don't believe them, There will be no age to come;

Ma - ny on the gold - en al - tar, "Purified, made white and tried"
When the sev-enth trumpet thunders, Then shall time no lon-ger' be.
When with fire the heav'ns are burning, And the earth shall be destroyed,
If in life you find not Je - sus, Death will seal your awful doom.

No. 100. Love is Freedom's Law.

D. S. WARNER. (Jer. 31:3.) AMANDA L. SPECK.

1. O love divine, un-fath-omed! O shore-less sea of bliss! Thy throne the highest heaven, Yet flowing down to this Dark world of guilt and sor-row, Redeems the fettered soul, Thy paths of peace I follow; O love, our hearts extol!
2. Enshrined with-in the bo-som Of Fa-ther's tender love, We seem in deep mid-o-cean Of heaven's bliss a-bove. Oh, wonders of re-demp-tion! We gaze in si-lent awe Up-on the new cre-a-tion, Where love is freedom's law.
3. Worlds of ex-tat-ic glo-ry, Love o-pens to our view, Where saints and an-gels tru-ly Find joys for-ev-er new. Sweet el-e-ment of heav-en! He is supreme-ly blest, Who, in thy sea o'er-whelmed, Has found e-ter-nal rest.
4. Love holds a roy-al scep-ter, And Mer-cy looketh down, Both call-ing to the sin-ner:"Come, wear a star-ry crown." Oh, sweet di-vine com-pas-sion! Poor sinner, taste and see, If grace thy heart may fash-ion; Then love shall reign in thee.

CHORUS.

O love! supreme affection! We bow low at thy shrine, Love is our great salvation; O love di-vine!

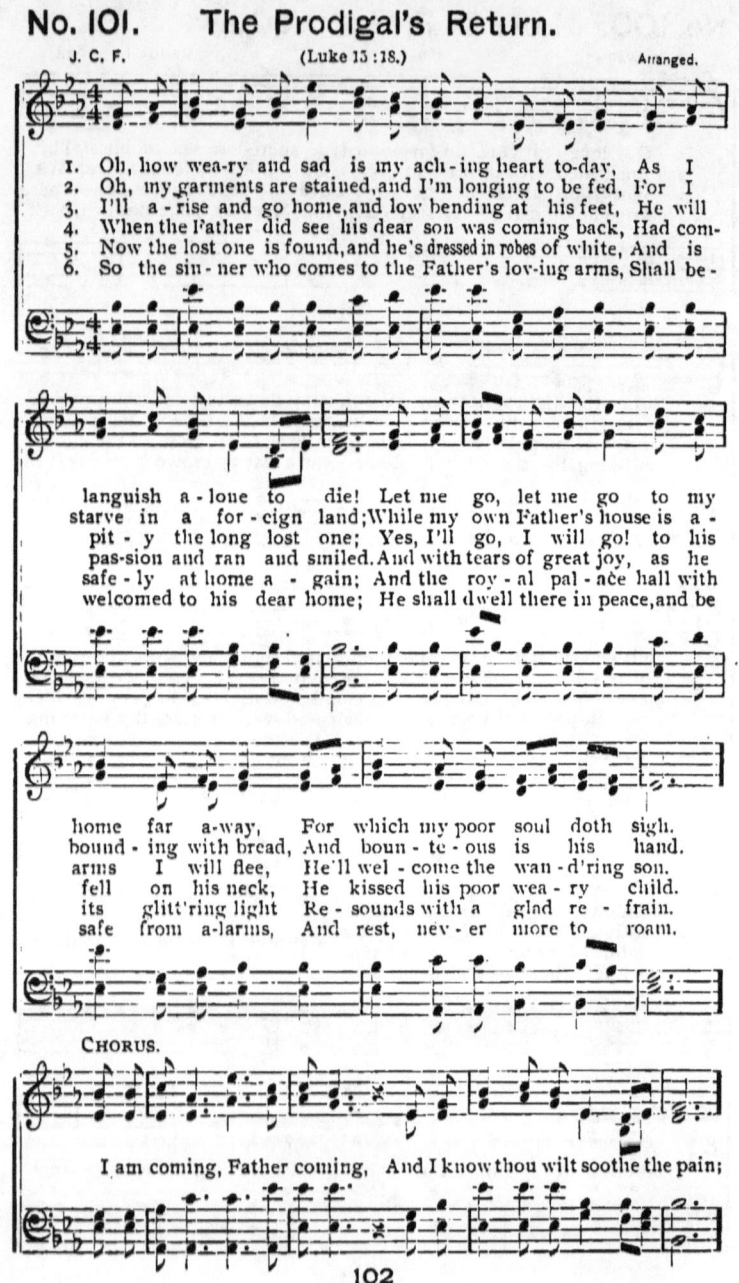

The Prodigal's Return. Concluded.

And my poor throbbing heart with joy shall sing, When the wand'rer's home a-gain.

No. 102. Don't Resist the Holy Spirit.

D S. W *Not too fast.* (Acts 7:51.) J. C. F.

1. Don't re-sist the Ho-ly Spir-it, Sin-ner, heed his lov-ing voice;
2. Don't re-sist the Ho-ly Spir-it, For he comes to save thy soul;
3. Don't re-sist the Ho-ly Spir-it, Do not grieve the gentle Dove;
4. Don't re-sist the Ho-ly Spir-it, He has called you oft be-fore;

Oh, in-vite him to thy bosom, Peace shall crown that blessed choice.
Taste his love so pure-ly giv-en, Humbly yield to his con-trol.
He will wit-ness sins for-giv-en, And the bliss of per-fect love.
This may be his fi-nal vis-it, If you o-pen not the door.

CHORUS.

Come, poor sin-ner, yield to Je-sus, At his throne of mer-cy bow;

Oh, the Spir-it bids you welcome, Come, and he will save you now.

No. 110. **There's Only One.**

JAS McGRANAHAN.

1. There's on - ly One whose pit - y falls, Like dew upon the wounded heart;
2. There's on - ly One who's never harsh, But ten-der-ness it-self to all;
3. There's on - ly One who can support, And who sufficient grace can give;
4. Oh, bless-ed Je - sus, Friend of friends, Come, hide us 'neath thy shelt'ring arm,
5. Thou art the One, the on - ly one For whom no love too warm can flow;

There's on - ly One who nev - er stirs, Tho' en - e-my and friend depart.
There's on - ly One who knows each heart, And list - ens to its faintest call.
To bear up un - der ev - 'ry grief, And spotless in this world to live.
Come down a-mid this wicked world, And keep us from its guilt and harm.
Thou art the One, the on - ly one, In whom there's perfect rest below.

CHORUS.

There's on - ly One, there's on-ly One, Can make us tru-ly, tru-ly blest;

There's on - ly One, there's on-ly One, Can give us perfect, perfect rest.

No. III. Hope of the Righteous.

LUELLA BYERS HENRY. (Tit. 2:13.) JOHN S. BYERS

Not too slow.

1. Be-yond this world of toil and care, Be-yond this veil of gloom;
2. Oh, what a bless-ed hope is this, An an-chor to the soul;
3. God says, "Ye must be born again;" To us this truth is given;
4. To en-ter heav'n we must be pure And ho-ly in his sight;
5. We'll pray for God to keep our feet Up-on the Cor-ner Stone;

There is a land, a hap-py land, A place we call our home.
And if we do our Sav-ior's will, We'll safe-ly reach the goal.
And if we do not his commands, We shall not en-ter heav'n.
And ev-'ry day we sure-ly must Be walk-ing in the light.
We'll give our hearts and lives to him, For we are not our own.

CHORUS.

Oh, yes, we'll trust him while we live! We'll trust him when we die;

rit.

And then when all our work is done, We'll reign with him on high.

Will You Come? Concluded.

Will you come to our dear Sav-ior? Will you come? he'll set you free:

No. 116. Beautiful Christ.

B. E. WARREN. (Psa. 87:3.) Arr. by B. E. W.

1. Beau-ti-ful *Christ;* a Sav-ior true, To all who come to him;
2. Beau-ti-ful *Word,* glad tidings giv'n, To Ad-am's fall-en race;
3. Beau-ti-ful *Light,* for-ev-er shine Up-on my path-way here;
4. Beau-ti-ful *Life,* how sweet to know 'Tis hid with Christ in God;

Will you be saved among the "few," From ev'ry stain of sin?
Guiding us home from earth to heav'n, Where we shall see his face.
Fill-ing my heart with joy sublime, My ransomed soul to cheer.
He's guid-ing our foot-steps here be-low, In the path that Je-sus trod.

CHORUS.

Beau - - ti-ful *Christ,*...... Beau - - ti-ful *Word,*......
Beau-ti-ful, beau-ti-ful, beau-ti-ful *Christ,* Beau-ti-ful, beau-ti-ful, beau-ti-ful *Word.*

rit.

Beau-ti-ful *Light* of the gos-pel, And beautiful *Life* of God.

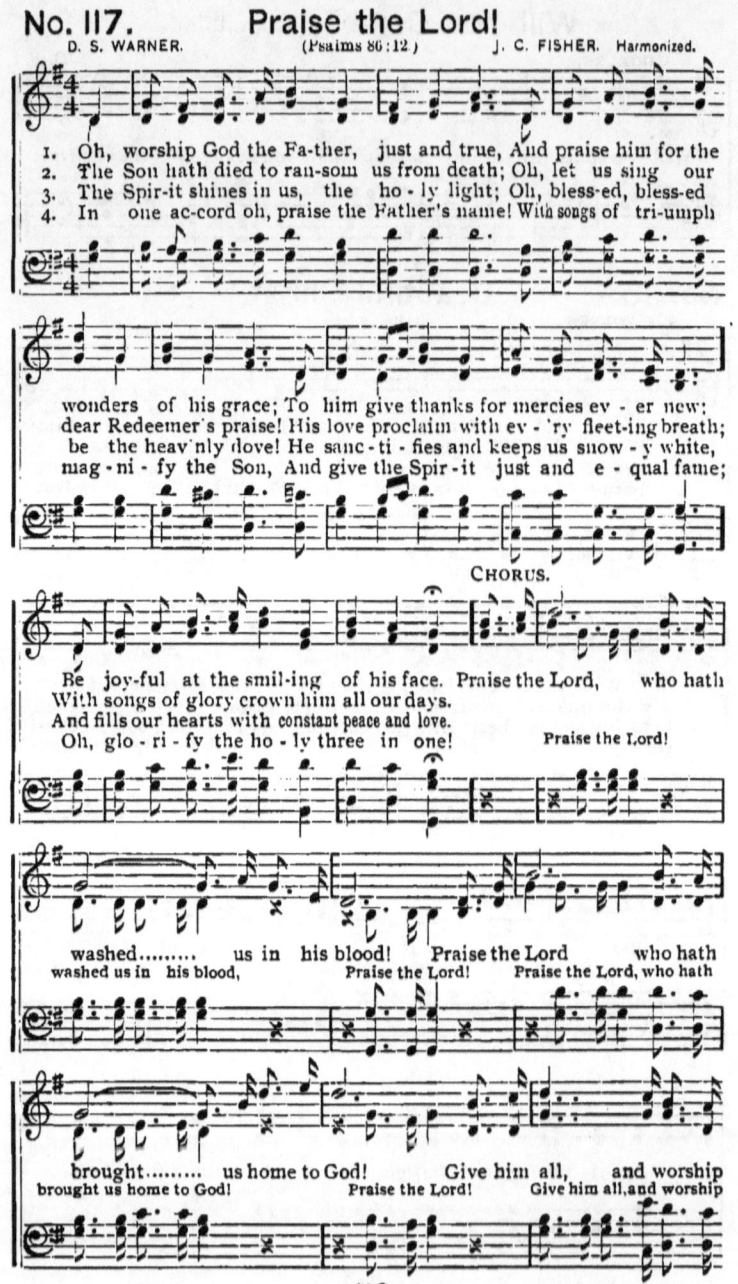

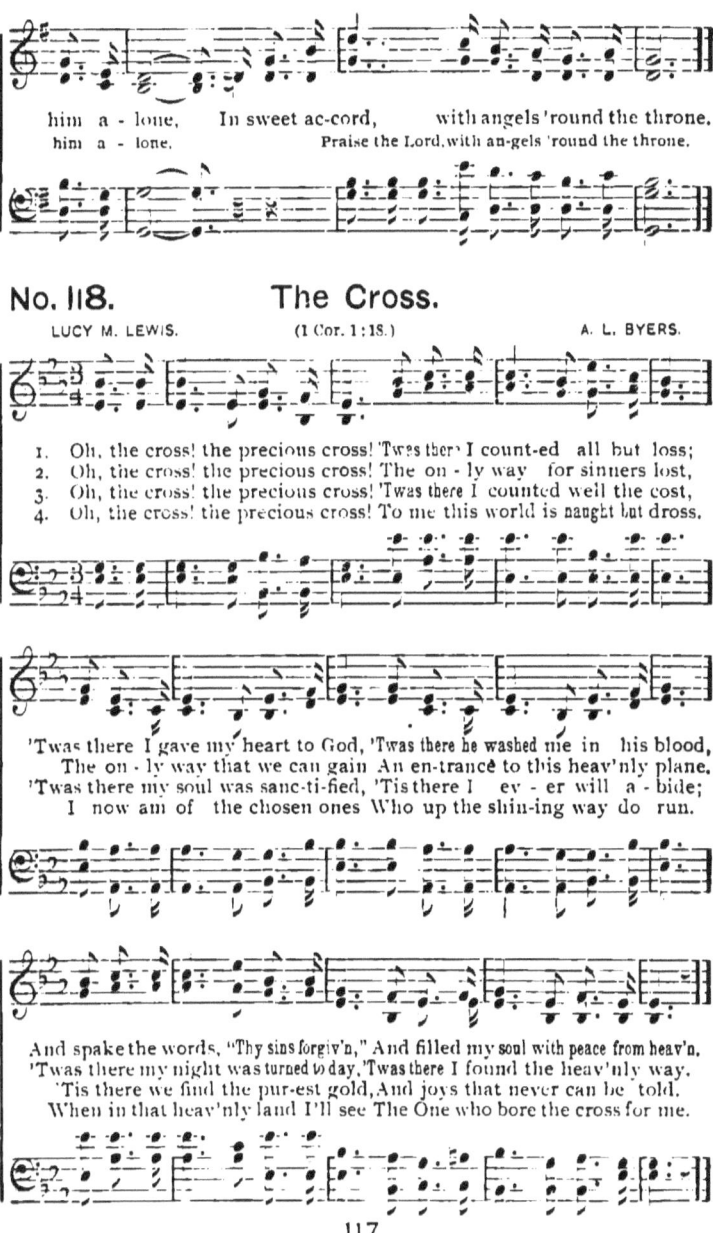

Praise the Lord! Concluded.

him a-lone, In sweet ac-cord, with angels 'round the throne.
him a-lone. Praise the Lord, with an-gels 'round the throne.

No. 118. The Cross.

LUCY M. LEWIS.   (1 Cor. 1:18.)   A. L. BYERS.

1. Oh, the cross! the precious cross! 'Twas there I count-ed all but loss;
2. Oh, the cross! the precious cross! The on-ly way for sinners lost,
3. Oh, the cross! the precious cross! 'Twas there I counted well the cost,
4. Oh, the cross! the precious cross! To me this world is naught but dross.

'Twas there I gave my heart to God, 'Twas there he washed me in his blood,
The on-ly way that we can gain An en-trance to this heav'nly plane.
'Twas there my soul was sanc-ti-fied, 'Tis there I ev-er will a-bide;
I now am of the chosen ones Who up the shin-ing way do run.

And spake the words, "Thy sins forgiv'n," And filled my soul with peace from heav'n.
'Twas there my night was turned to day, 'Twas there I found the heav'nly way.
'Tis there we find the pur-est gold, And joys that never can be told.
When in that heav'nly land I'll see The One who bore the cross for me.

Table Hymn. Concluded.

'Tis from thy hand of love divine, We feed once more these bod-ies, thine.
We eat and live to God a-lone, Who makes our hearts his bliss-ful throne.

No. 121.   Come, Jesus, Reign in Me.

H. R. J.   (John 14:23)   H. R. J.

1. For per-fect love I long have groaned, I would be whol-ly thine;
2. All foes cast out, let this poor heart Be filled with love di-vine;
3. Let per-fect love my por-tion be, To thee my all re-sign;
4. No earth-ly language can express The love in Christ I find;

Yes, I would have the Lord enthron'd In this poor heart of mine.
Se-cure-ly fixed, no more to part From this poor heart of mine.
O Ho-ly One, come dwell in me, And rule this heart of mine.
'Tis boundless and it's meas-ure-less, In this poor heart of mine.

CHORUS.

Come, Je-sus, reign in me,   My heart thy throne shall be;

Oh, tar-ry in thy throne, 'Tis thine and thine a-lone.

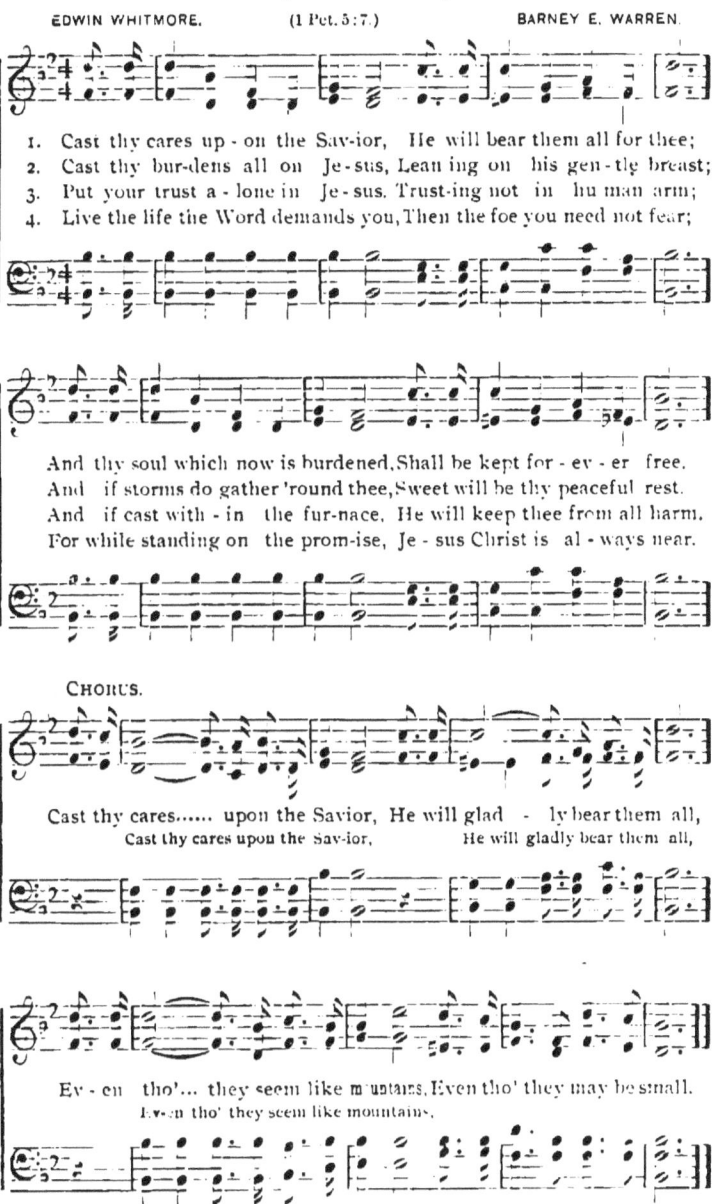

Reigning in this Life. Concluded.

No. 125. I've Touched the Hem of His Garment.

(Matt. 9:21.)   Words and Music arranged.

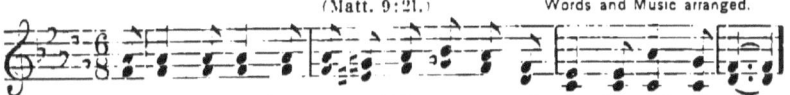

1. In faith she touched the hem of his garment, As to his side she stole,
2. She came with fear and trembling before him. She knew the Lord had come,
3. He turned with, "Daughter, be of good comfort, Thy faith hath made thee whole."

A-mid the crowd that gather'd around him, And straightway she was whole.
She felt that from him virtue had heal'd her. The mighty deed was done.
And peace which passeth all understanding, With gladness filled her soul.

CHORUS

I've touched the hem of his garment, And now I too am free;

His healing pow'r this ver-y hour, Gives life and health to me.

I Never Shall Forget. Concluded.

done for me, Is do-ing for me yet. I nev-er shall for-get, I never shall forget, What Je-sus Christ has done for me, Is do-ing for me yet.

No. 127. I Am Free.
Words and Music by J. C. FISHER.   (John 8:36.)   Harmonized.

1. I am free, the Lord hath sav'd me, I was burdened with my sin;
2. In his pit-y he redeem'd me, When he saw me in my woe;
3. Oh, the gush-ing springs of glo-ry, That are flooding all my heart;
4. Oh, the joy, no tongue can tell it, 'Tis like ma-ny flowing streams;

FINE.

Then he whisper'd meek and lowly: "Come to me, I'll take you in."
Yes, he sanc-ti-fied and cleansed me, And I'm whit-er than the snow.
And the mu-sic sweet and heav'nly, Wakes the chords in ev-'ry part.
Now I stand up-on the sum-mit, Where the gold-en sunlight gleams.

D. S.—*I will tell the wondrous sto-ry, Of the blood that cleanseth me.*

CHORUS.   D. S.

Hal - le - lu - jah! glo-ry! glo - ry! Let us sound the ju - bi - lee.

The Hand of God on the Wall. Concluded.

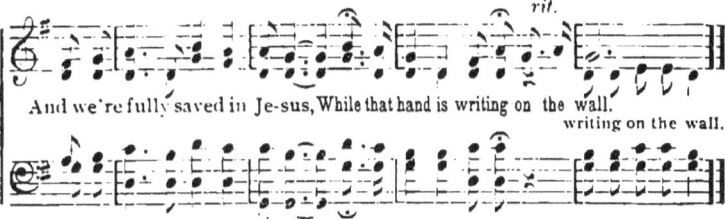

And we're fully saved in Je-sus, While that hand is writing on the wall,
writing on the wall.

5 Hear the loud voice from heaven, "Come, my people, gather home!"
For to you the signs are given, that the Lord is near to come:
Now he shakes every nation, heed the warning, great and small,
For the wicked soon shall perish, says the hand upon the wall.

6 See the saints come to Zion and possess the holy land!
Hallelujah! shout the freedom! in the living God we stand.
Since we follow the Savior, love and serve him Lord of all.
Babel's kingdom now is finished, says the hand upon the wall.

No. 135.   All to Thee.

JAMES L. BLACK.   JNO. R. SWENEY.

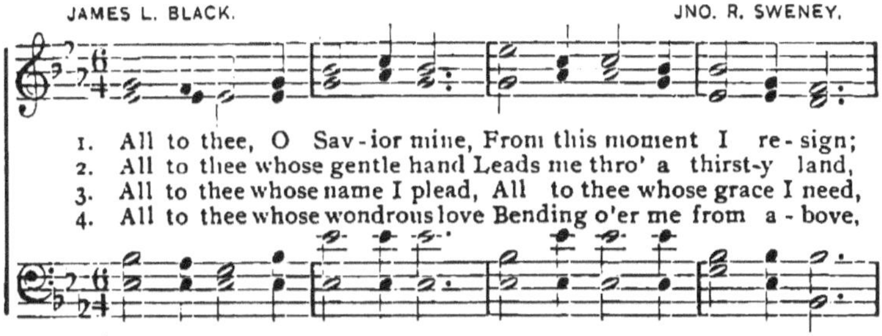

1. All to thee, O Sav-ior mine, From this moment I re-sign;
2. All to thee whose gentle hand Leads me thro' a thirst-y land,
3. All to thee whose name I plead, All to thee whose grace I need,
4. All to thee whose wondrous love Bending o'er me from a-bove,

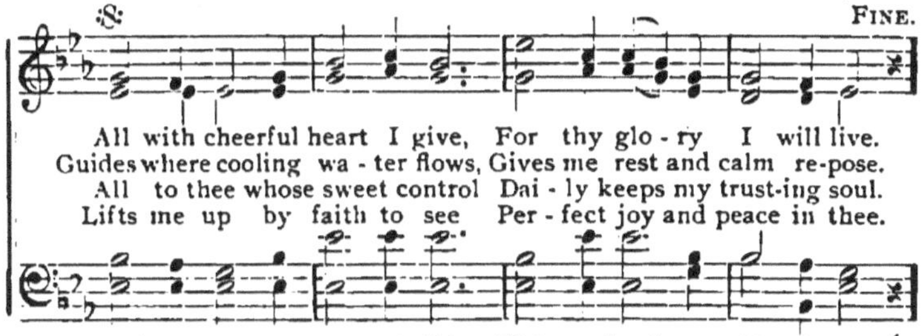

All with cheerful heart I give, For thy glo-ry I will live.
Guides where cooling wa-ter flows, Gives me rest and calm re-pose.
All to thee whose sweet control Dai-ly keeps my trust-ing soul.
Lifts me up by faith to see Per-fect joy and peace in thee.

D. S.—*This my fer-vent pray'r shall be, Hide, O Lord, my life with thee.*

REFRAIN.

All to thee, all to thee, Thou hast shed thy blood for me,

From "Glad Hallelujahs," by per.

I'll Enter the Open Door. Concluded.

'Tis Je - sus in-vites, I'll en - ter in, I'll en-ter the o - pen door.

No. 139. How Firm a Foundation.

Arranged.

1. How firm a foun-da-tion, ye saints of the Lord, Is laid for your
2. Fear not, I am with thee; oh, be not dismayed: For I am thy
3. When thro' fier-y tri - als thy pathway shall lie, My grace all suf -
4. The soul that on Je-sus doth lean for re - pose, I will not, I

faith in his ex - cel-lent word! What more can he say than to
God, and will still give thee aid: I'll strengthen thee, help thee, and
fi-cient shall be thy sup-ply; The flame shall not harm thee, I
will not de - sert to his foes; That soul, tho' all hell should en-

you he hath said, Ye, who un-to Je - sus for ref - uge have fled?
cause thee to stand, Up-held by my righteous om - nip - o-tent hand.
on - ly de - sign Thy dross to con-sume, and thy gold to re - fine.
deav - or to shake, I'll nev - er, no, nev - er, no, nev - er for - sake.

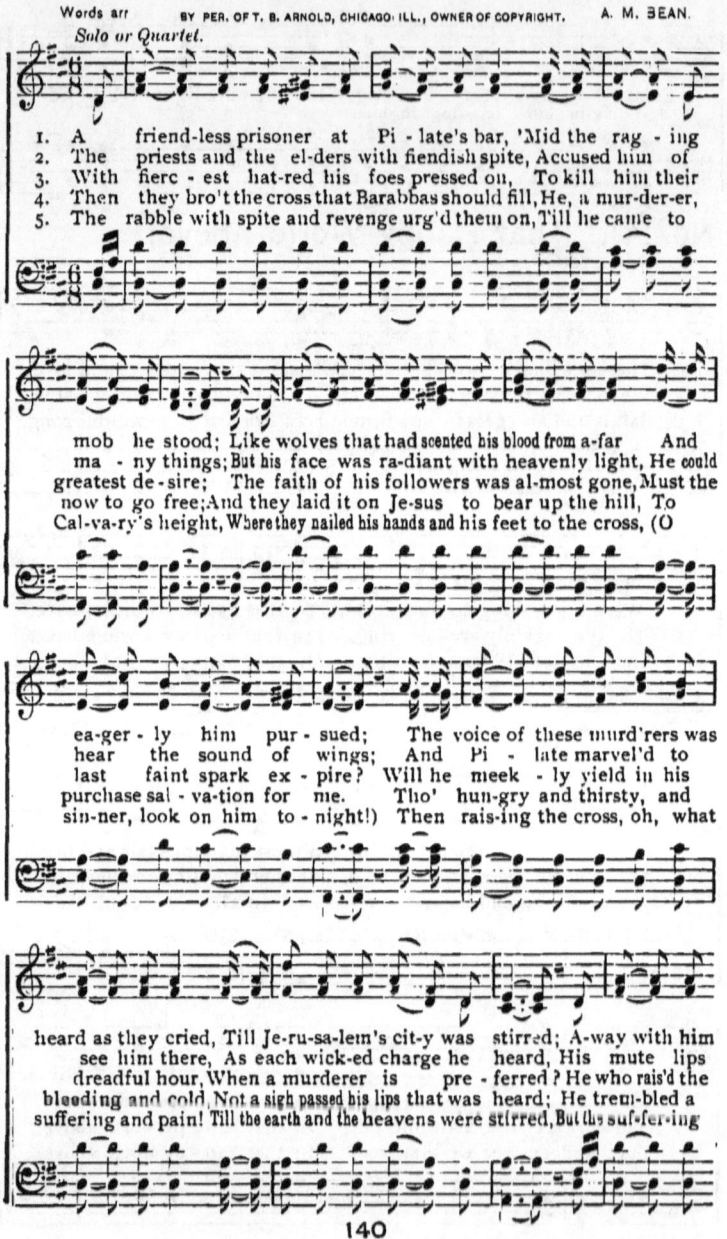

He Answered Never a Word. Concluded.

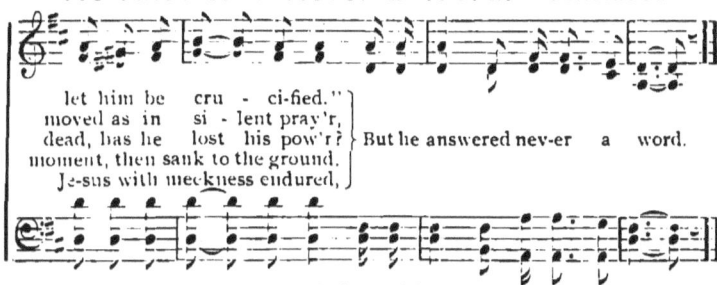

let him be cru - ci-fied."
moved as in si - lent pray'r,
dead, has he lost his pow'r?
moment, then sank to the ground.
Je-sus with meekness endured,

But he answered nev-er a word.

6. But there hung by his side a thief, broken and sad,
With sins that were all his own,
And he cried; "Dear Lord, remember me
When thou sittest on thy throne "
And the Savior turned and looked upon him,
His compassion deep was stirred;
And peace, sweet peace he shed o'er that soul—
He could answer him with a word.

No. 143. It is better Farther On.

Words and Music .. tr. L. THOMPSON.

1. Hark! I hear hope sweetly singing Soft-ly in an un - der-tone,
2. When my faith took hold on Jesus, Light di-vine with-in me shone,
3. Far - ther on, but how much farther? Count the mile-stones one by one;

Sing-ing as if God had taught her, "It is bet-ter far - ther on."
D. S.–Singing so my heart may hear it, "It is bet ter far - ther on."
And I know since that glad moment, "It is bet ter far - ther on."
D. S.–I am saved and Hope , is singing, "It is bet-ter far - ther on."
No, no counting, on - ly trusting—"It is bet-ter far - ther on."
D. S.–Je - sus is my Sav-ior, keep-er,—"It is bet-ter far - ther on."

Night and day I hear her singing,—Singing while I sit a - lone,
I have plung'd in-to the fountain, Flow-ing free for ev - 'ry one;
Rest, my soul, in hope for-ev - er, All my doubts and fears are gone;

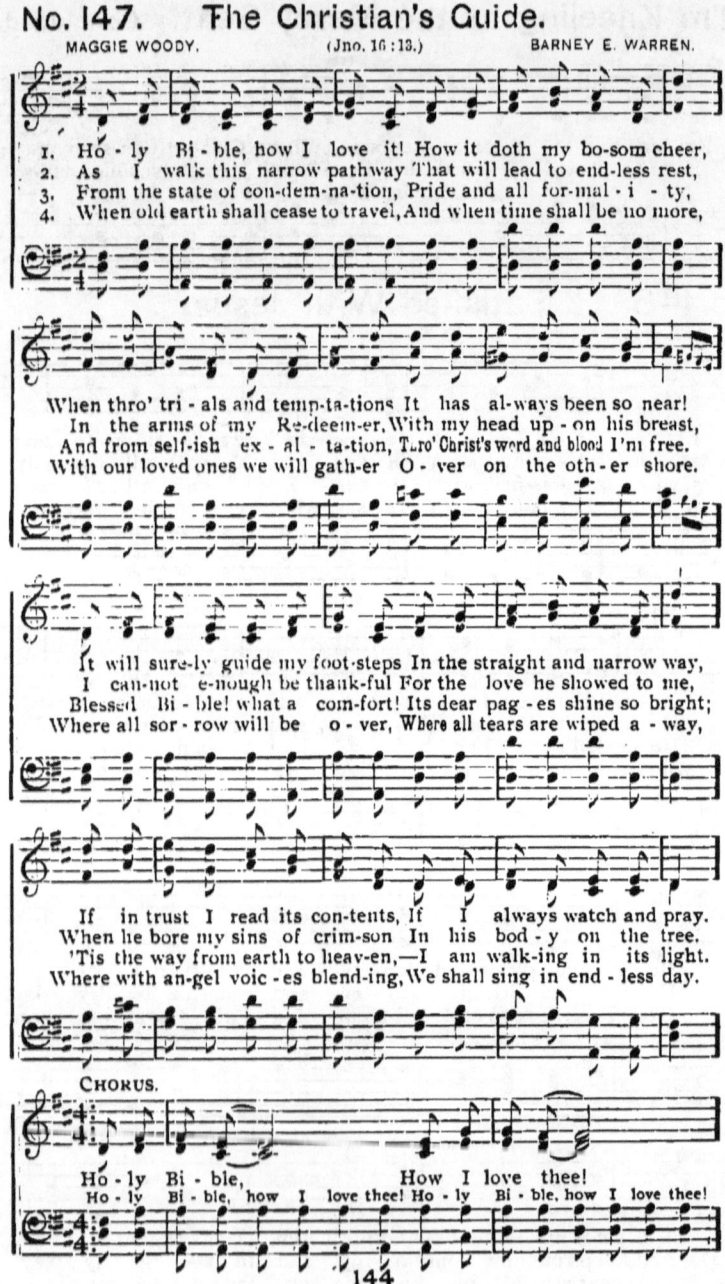

The Christian's Guide. Concluded.

Saf-est guide thro' this dark world; See its ban-ner now un-furled.

No. 148. Little Pilgrims.

NORA SIENS HUNTER. C. E. HUNTER.

1. I am on-ly a lit-tle sail-or, To stem the rag-ing tide,
2. I am on-ly a lit-tle sol-dier, To fight in this great war,
3. I am on-ly a lit-tle Chris-tian, To walk at Je-sus' side,

But I will not shrink or fal-ter, For Je-sus is my guide;
But I will not fear or trem-ble, Nor give the bat-tle o'er;
But I'll fol-low where he leads me, What-ev-er may be-tide;

Tho' the waves may dash a-round me, The winds may fiercely roar,
And tho' war should rise a-gainst me, My soul to o-ver-throw,
Tho' the world may try to win me, With pleasures rich and gay,

I will keep my eyes on Je-sus, And trust him ev-er-more.
I will brave-ly strug-gle on-ward, And con-quer ev-'ry foe.
I will trust in God my Sav-ior, He'll keep me day by day.

No. 155. O Save Me at the Cross.

FANNY J. CROSBY. (ALTAR SONG.) Arr.

1. Lov - ing Sav-ior, hear my cry, hear my cry, hear my cry;
2. I have sinn'd, but thou hast died, thou hast died, thou hast died;
3. Tho' I per - ish, I will pray, I will pray, I will pray;
4. Thou hast said thy grace is free, grace is free, grace is free;
5. Wash me in thy cleans-ing blood, cleansing blood, cleansing blood;
6. On - ly faith will par - don bring, par-don bring, par-don bring;

Tremb-ling to thy arms I fly, O save me at the cross.
In thy mer-cy let me hide, O save me at the cross.
Thou of life the liv - ing way, O save me at the cross.
Have com - pas-sion, Lord, on me, O save me at the cross.
Plunge me now be-neath the flood, O save me at the cross.
In that faith to thee I cling, O save me at the cross.

CHORUS.

Dear Je - sus, re - ceive me, No more would I grieve thee;

Repeat chorus pp.

Now, bless-ed Re - deem - er, O save me at the cross.

The River of Pleasure. Concluded.

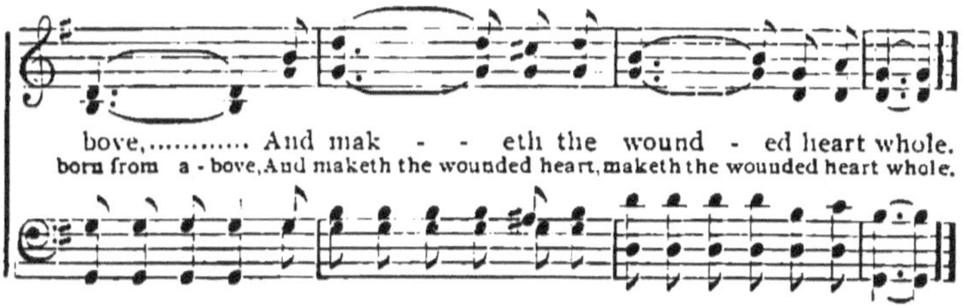

bove,............ And mak - - eth the wound - ed heart whole.
born from a - bove, And maketh the wounded heart, maketh the wounded heart whole.

No. 157.   Ever Lead Me.

B E. W.   (Psa. 139:10.)   BARNEY E. WARREN.

slow with expression.

1. Out on this dark world, Sav-ior, am I;   Be thou my help-er,
2. Hope of my heart, Lord, Strength of my soul, Guide thou my foot-steps,
3. Calm thou the wild storm, Clear up the way;   Keep me from fall-ing

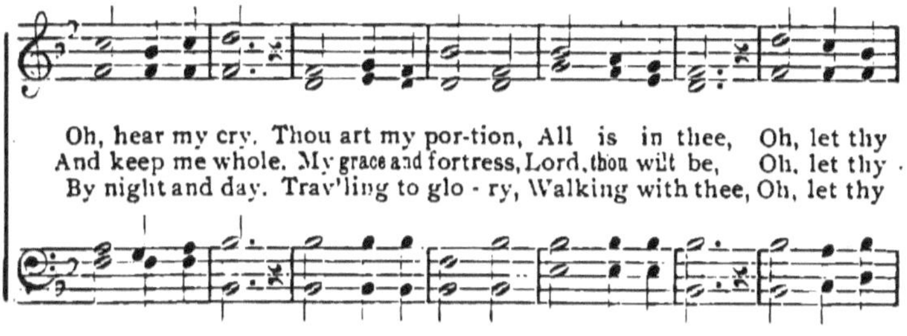

Oh, hear my cry, Thou art my por-tion, All is in thee, Oh, let thy
And keep me whole. My grace and fortress, Lord, thou wilt be,   Oh, let thy
By night and day. Trav'ling to glo - ry, Walking with thee, Oh, let thy

REFRAIN. *pp.*

might - y hand ev - er lead me.
might - y hand ev - er lead me.   Wilt thou lead me by thy hand?
might - y hand ev - er lead me.

B E. W., Springfield, O,

Perishing Souls. Concluded.

souls............ ... all this world be-side? Oh, who will help to save the lost? *rit.*
help to save the lost?
souls at stake to-day,

No. 163. I Know My Name is There.

D. S. WARNER.   (Luke 10:20.)   B. E. WARREN.

1. My name is in the book of Life, Oh, bless the name of Je-sus!
2. My name once stood with sinners, lost, And bore a pain-ful rec-ord;
3. Yet inward troub-le oft-en cast A shad-ow o'er my ti-tle;
4. While others climb thro' worldly strife, To carve a name of hon-or,

I rise a-bove all doubt and strife, And read my ti-tle clear.
But by his blood the Sav-ior cross'd, And placed it on his roll.
But now with full sal-va-tion blest, Praise God! it's ev-er clear.
High up in heaven's book of Life, My name is writ-ten there.

CHORUS.

I know,...... I know... my name...... is there;...
I know, I tru-ly know, I know my name is there;

I know,...... I know,......... my name is writ-ten there.
I know my name is there,

No. 170. Lost Forever.

B. E. W. — B. E. WARREN.

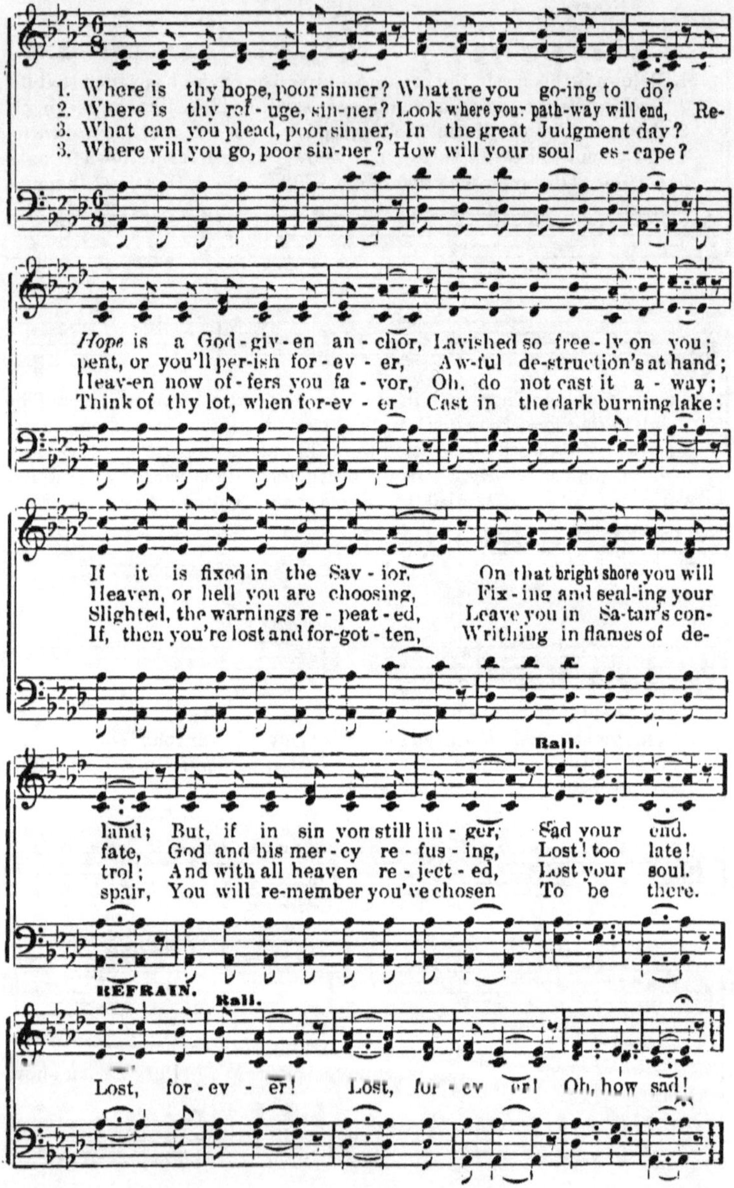

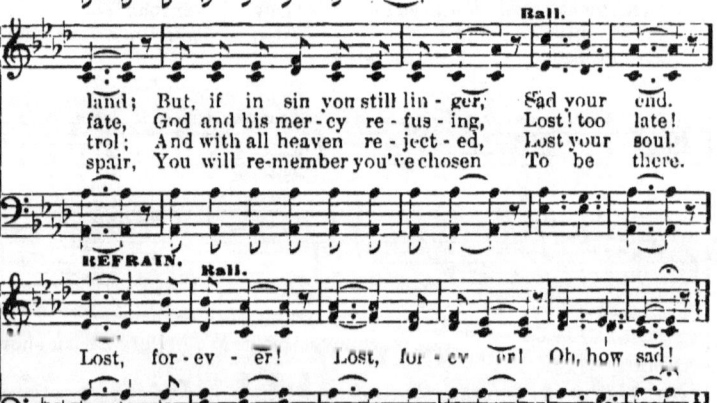

No. 171. Jesus is Pleading for Thee.

B. E. W. B. E. WARREN.

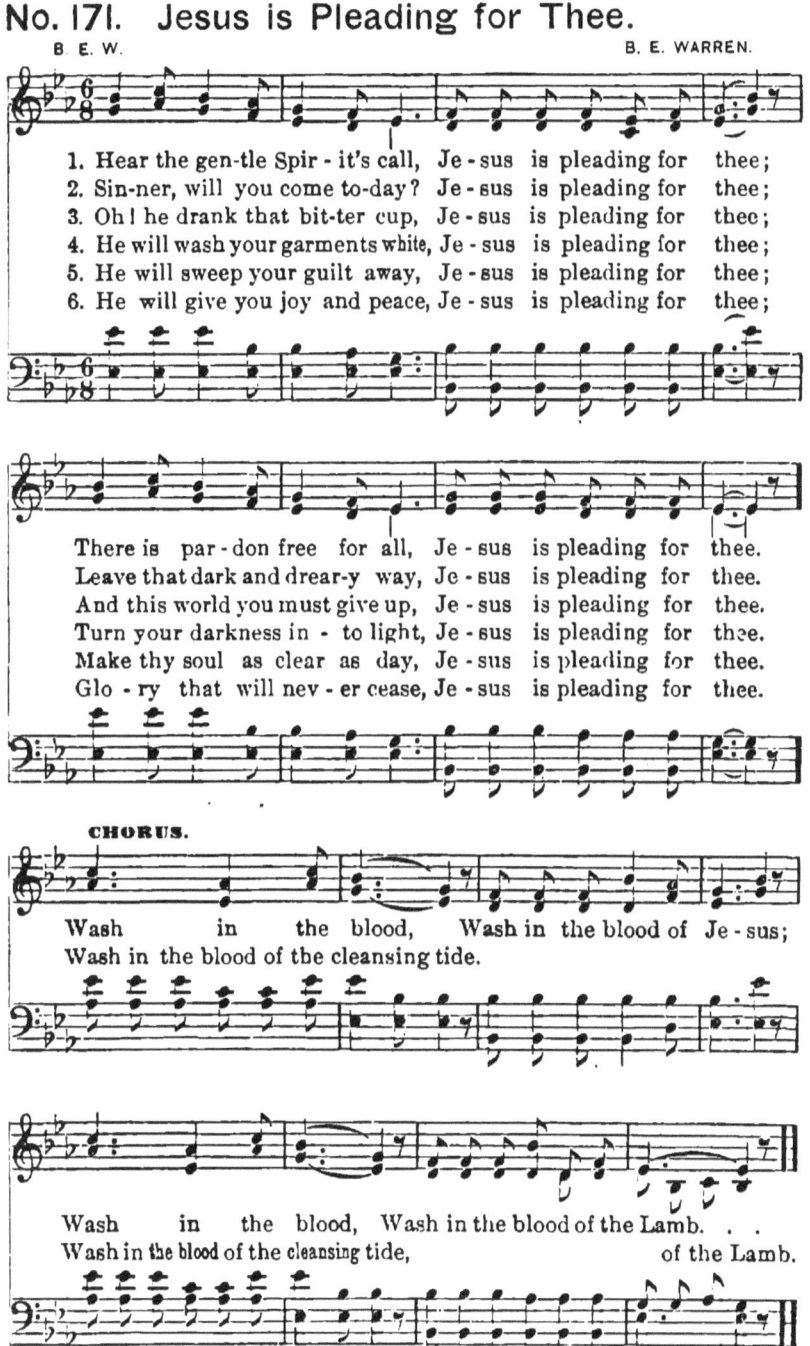

1. Hear the gen-tle Spir - it's call, Je-sus is pleading for thee;
2. Sin-ner, will you come to-day? Je-sus is pleading for thee;
3. Oh! he drank that bit-ter cup, Je-sus is pleading for thee;
4. He will wash your garments white, Je-sus is pleading for thee;
5. He will sweep your guilt away, Je-sus is pleading for thee;
6. He will give you joy and peace, Je-sus is pleading for thee;

There is par - don free for all, Je-sus is pleading for thee.
Leave that dark and drear-y way, Je-sus is pleading for thee.
And this world you must give up, Je-sus is pleading for thee.
Turn your darkness in - to light, Je-sus is pleading for thee.
Make thy soul as clear as day, Je-sus is pleading for thee.
Glo - ry that will nev - er cease, Je-sus is pleading for thee.

CHORUS.

Wash in the blood, Wash in the blood of Je-sus;
Wash in the blood of the cleansing tide.

Wash in the blood, Wash in the blood of the Lamb. . .
Wash in the blood of the cleansing tide, of the Lamb.

No. 175. The Church Triumphant.

D. S. WARNER. (2 Cor. 2:14.) B. E. WARREN.

1. Men speak of a *"Church triumphant,"* As something on earth unknown,
2. Oh, can not the great Redeem-er Pre-vail o-ver Sa-tan here?
3. He built on a sure founda-tion, And said that the gates of hell,
4. Then how can you say, dear people, You can not be kept each day?
5. 'Tis not in the Church of Je-sus, That people yet live in sin;
6. God's Church is alone triumphant, In ho-li-ness all com-plete;

They think us beneath the ty-rant, Un-til we shall reach our home.
Or must we re-main yet un-der Con-fusion, pressed down in fear?
A-gainst her di-vine mu-ni-tion, Can nev-er in-deed pre-vail.
The In-fi-nite arm is a-ble, His word has not passed a-way.
But in the dark creeds they're joining, And vainly are trusting in.
And all the dark pow'rs of Sa-tan, She tramples beneath her feet.

CHORUS.

Thank God for a "Church triumphant," All pure in this world be-low;

For the kingdom that Je-sus founded, Does triumph o'er ev'ry foe.

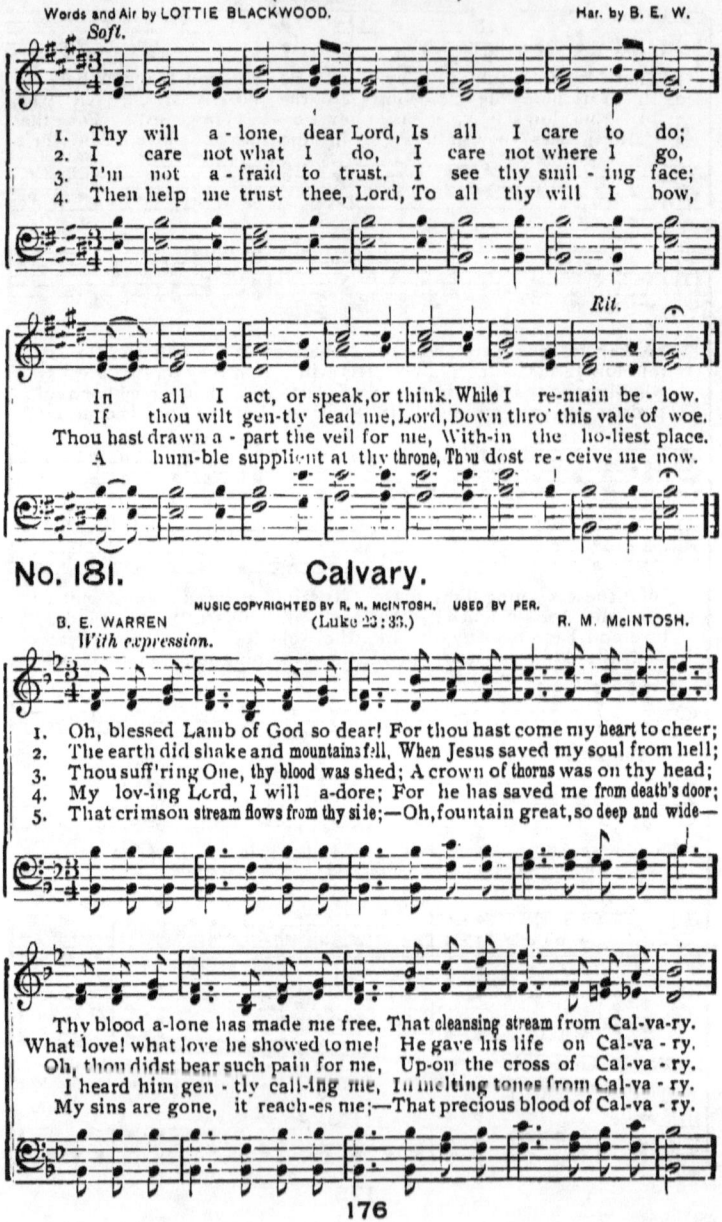

Calvary. Concluded.

{ O Calvary! dark Calvary! There Jesus bore the cross for me; }
{ O Calvary! dark Calvary! Hark! (*Omit.*) } hear him groan for you and me.

No. 182. Only One Narrow Way.

B. E. F.   (John 14:6; 10:9.)   Melody by BIRDIE E FINK.
Har. by B. E. W.

Slow, with expression.

1. On - ly one nar-row way, "I am the way;" On - ly one
2. On - ly one mind and mouth, all speak the same, On - ly one
3. Oh, see his crimson blood, flow - ing for all; Be-hold thy

o-pen door, "I am the door;" On-ly one Shepherd kind, to heal the
Church of God, kept in his name; On-ly one gentle hand to lead the
patient Friend drinking life's gall; On-ly one rest complete, low at his

sick and blind; On - ly one reeking cross for souls that are lost.
lit - tle band, On - ly one ho - ly plain, one heaven to gain.
love-ly feet, On - ly one fountain free, 'tis flow-ing for thee.

REFRAIN.   *Rit.*

Only one narrow way, "I am the way," Only one o-pen door, "I am the door."

No. 183. Come, While He is Calling.

N. H. BYRUM — B. E. WARREN.

1. If dear sin-ner, you are long-ing All those sinful chains to break,
2. O dear sin-ner, do not tar - ry, When your soul in per-il lies,
3. Turn, dear sinner, from the e-vils That have laden down your heart,

And re-lieve your soul from anguish, Which no human form can take,
Tho' your sins be great like mountains, Tow-'ring up-ward to the skies;
And have made your home un-hap-py,—'Tis the demon's fier-y dart.

Then de cide this ver - y moment, That from bondage you'll be free;
For, from ev - 'ry one he'll free you, And a ref - uge he will be;
Turn, oh, turn to Christ, our Sav-ior, And for him yield fruits of love,

Heed, oh, heed his woo-ing Spir - it, Come and he will par-don thee.
He's the bless-ed Rock of A - ges That was cleft for you and me.
Which will prove to all a bless-ing, And will crown your soul above.

CHORUS.

Then, oh, come, while he is call - ing, Lay your
Then, oh, come, while he is call-ing, Then, oh, come, while he is call-ing,

A Happy Band. Concluded.

all e-ter-ni-ty, From earth and sor-row free, where all is love.
sin each day and hour, Where blessings ev-er show'r from heav'n above.
forth God's only Son, For he the work hath done. Praise him to-day!
truth in evening light, With Satan's hosts to fight, then watch and pray.

No. 187. The Bondage of Love.

GEO. D. WATSON.   COPYRIGHT, 1895, BY E. A. HOFFMAN. BY PER.   JOSEPH GARRISON.

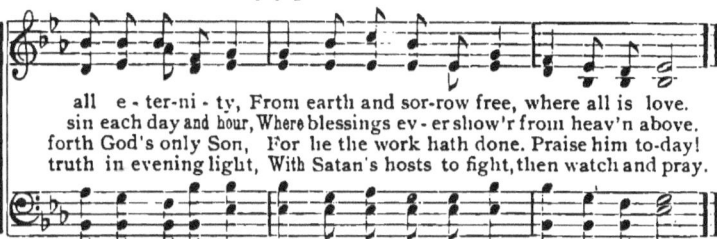

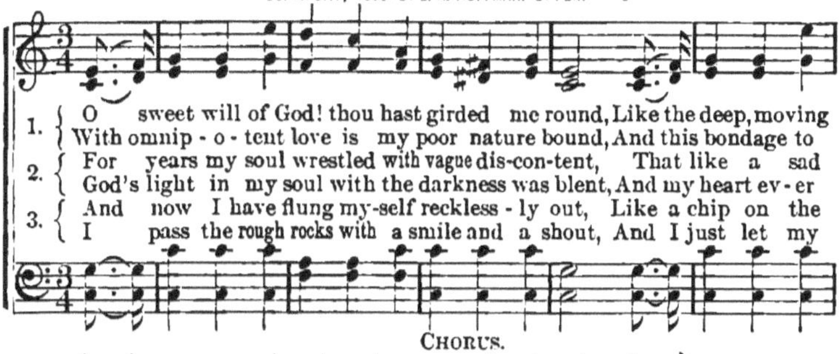

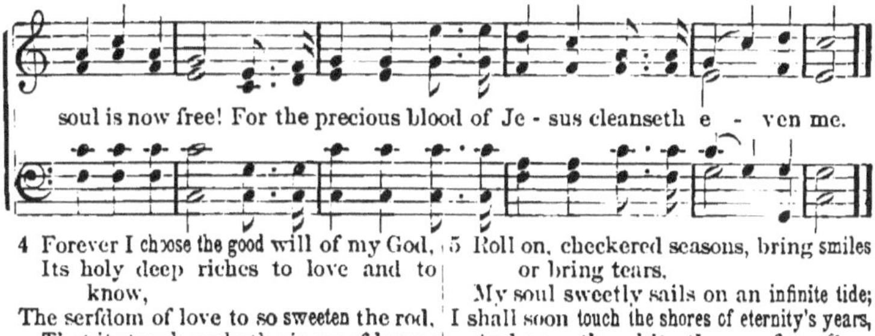

1. { O sweet will of God! thou hast girded me round, Like the deep, moving
   { With omnip-o-tent love is my poor nature bound, And this bondage to
2. { For years my soul wrestled with vague dis-con-tent, That like a sad
   { God's light in my soul with the darkness was blent, And my heart ev-er
3. { And now I have flung my-self reckless-ly out, Like a chip on the
   { I pass the rough rocks with a smile and a shout, And I just let my

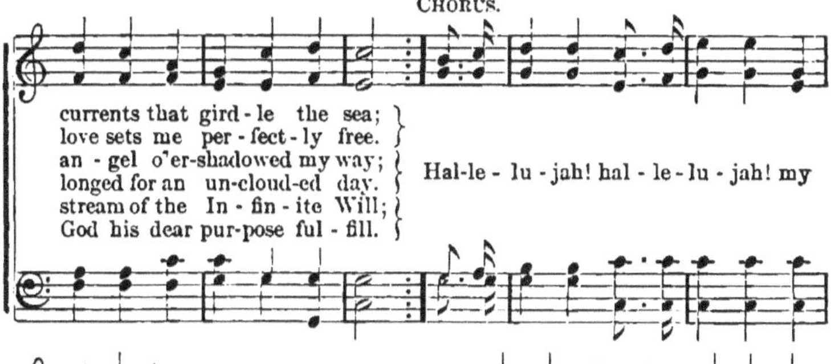

CHORUS.

currents that gird-le the sea; }
love sets me per-fect-ly free. }
an-gel o'er-shadowed my way; }   Hal-le-lu-jah! hal-le-lu-jah! my
longed for an un-cloud-ed day. }
stream of the In-fin-ite Will; }
God his dear pur-pose ful-fill. }

soul is now free! For the precious blood of Je-sus cleanseth e-ven me.

4 Forever I chose the good will of my God,
  Its holy deep riches to love and to know,
  The serfdom of love to so sweeten the rod,
  That its touch maketh rivers of honey to flow.

5 Roll on, checkered seasons, bring smiles or bring tears,
  My soul sweetly sails on an infinite tide;
  I shall soon touch the shores of eternity's years,
  And near the white throne of my Sav-ior abide.

No. 189. I Must Tell Jesus.

E. A. H. COPYRIGHT, 1893, BY THE HOFFMAN MUSIC CO. BY PER. ELISHA A. HOFFMAN.

1. I must tell Je-sus all of my tri-als; I can-not bear these burdens a-lone; In my distress he kind-ly will help me; He ev-er loves and cares for his own.
2. I must tell Je-sus all of my troub-les; He is a kind, com-passionate Friend; If I but ask him, he will de-liv-er, Make of my troub-les quick-ly an end.
3. Tempted and tried I need a great Sav-ior, One who can help my burdens to bear; I must tell Je-sus, I must tell Je-sus; He all my cares and sor-rows will share.

CHORUS.

I must tell Je-sus! I must tell Je-sus! I can-not bear my bur-dens a-lone; I must tell Je-sus! I must tell Je-sus! Je-sus can help me, Je-sus a-lone.

Rit.

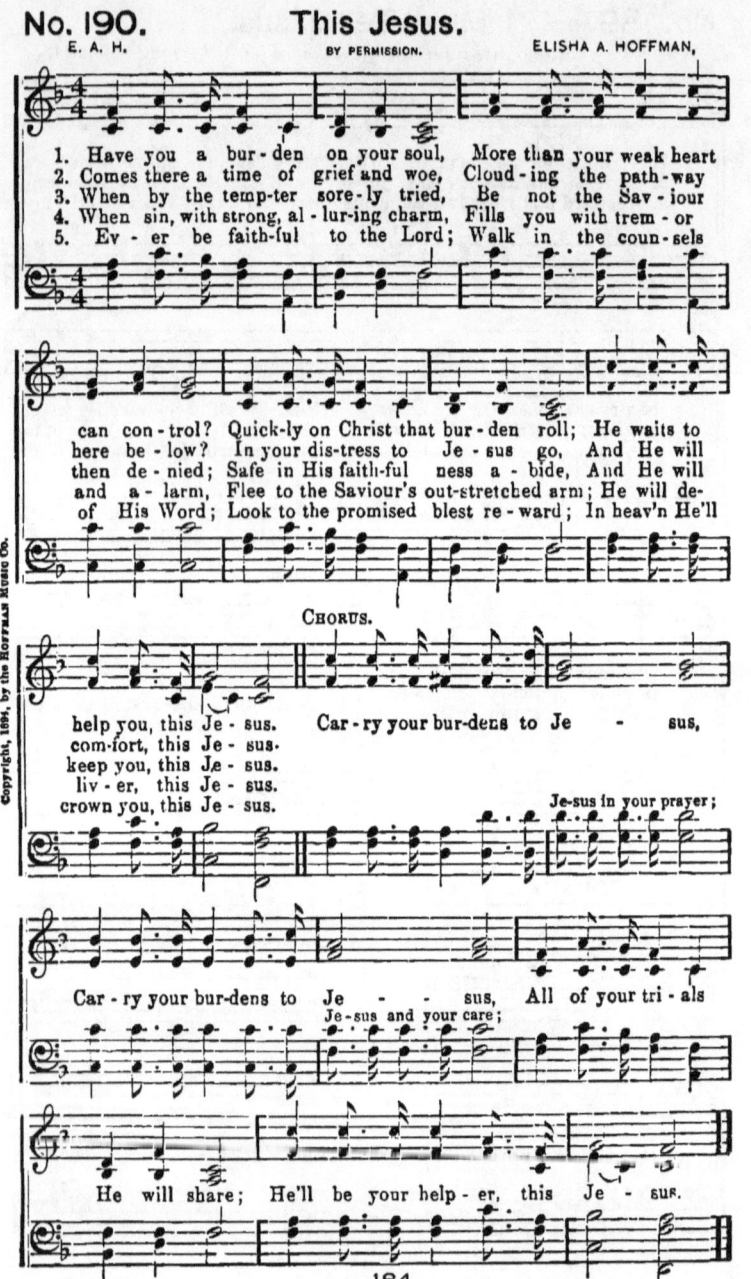

No. 191. That's Enough for Me.

COPYRIGHT, 1878, 1887, 1893, BY THE HOFFMAN MUSIC CO. BY PER.

E. A. H. ELISHA A. HOFFMAN.

1. O love sur-pass-ing knowledge! O, grace so full and free!
2. O won-der-ful sal-va-tion, That I should ransomed be!
3. O blood of Christ so pre-cious, That flows from Cal-va-ry!
4. O won-drous love of Je-sus! What love could sweeter be?
5. We live in sweet com-mun-ion, In bless-ed har-mo-ny;

I know that Je-sus loves me, And that's e-nough for me.
'Tis mine, this sweet as-sur-ance, And that's e-nough for me.
It cleans-es me com-plete-ly, And that's e-nough for me.
He keeps me saved and hap-py, And that's e-nough for me.
This, this is full sal-va-tion, And that's e-nough for me.

REFRAIN.

And that's e-nough for me, E-nough of joy for me;

I know that Je-sus loves me, And that's e-nough for me.
'Tis mine, this sweet as-sur-ance, And that's e-nough for me.
It cleans-es me com-plete-ly, And that's e-nough for me.
He keeps me saved and hap-py, And that's e-nough for me.
God's free and full sal-va-tion, Oh, that's e-nough for me.

6 The worldling seeks for pleasure,
In earthly vanity;
My treasures are in heaven,
And that's enough for me.
Cho. And that's enough for me,
Enough of joy for me;
My treasures are in heaven,
And that's enough for me.

7 When ends our toil and sorrow,
A better home I'll see,
And be with Christ forever,
And that's enough for me.
Cho. And that's enough for me,
Enough of joy for me;
To be with Christ forever,
Oh, that's enough for me!

No. 192. Where is My Wayward Boy?

B. E. W.
BARNEY E. WARREN.

1. Where is my way-ward boy to-night? Out in a world of care?
2. Where is my way-ward boy to-night? Off on the plains of woe,
3. Where is my way-ward boy to-night? Has he for-got-ten home?
4. Where is my way-ward boy to-night? Where will he lay his head?
5. Where is my way-ward boy to-night? Does he not care for me,—
6. Where is my way-ward boy to-night? Lord, do not let him stray;

Roving in sin,—how sad the sight! For-get-ting a mother's pray'r.
Grieving a lov-ing mother's heart? Oh, child, can you treat her so?
Oh, could he know the pray'rs and tears Of moth-er, so sad and lone!
Oh, is he suf-f'ring in the cold, No shelter, no home, nor bread?
Pleading in love to teach him right, While sitting up-on my knee?
Can he a moth-er's love re-quite, By sin-ning his life a-way?

CHORUS.

Where is my boy to-night?... Where is my boy to-night?...
Where is my way-ward boy to-night? Where is my way-ward boy to-night?

Where is my boy to-night?... Oh, where is my boy to-night?
Where is my way-ward boy to-night?

B. E. Warren, Springfield, O.

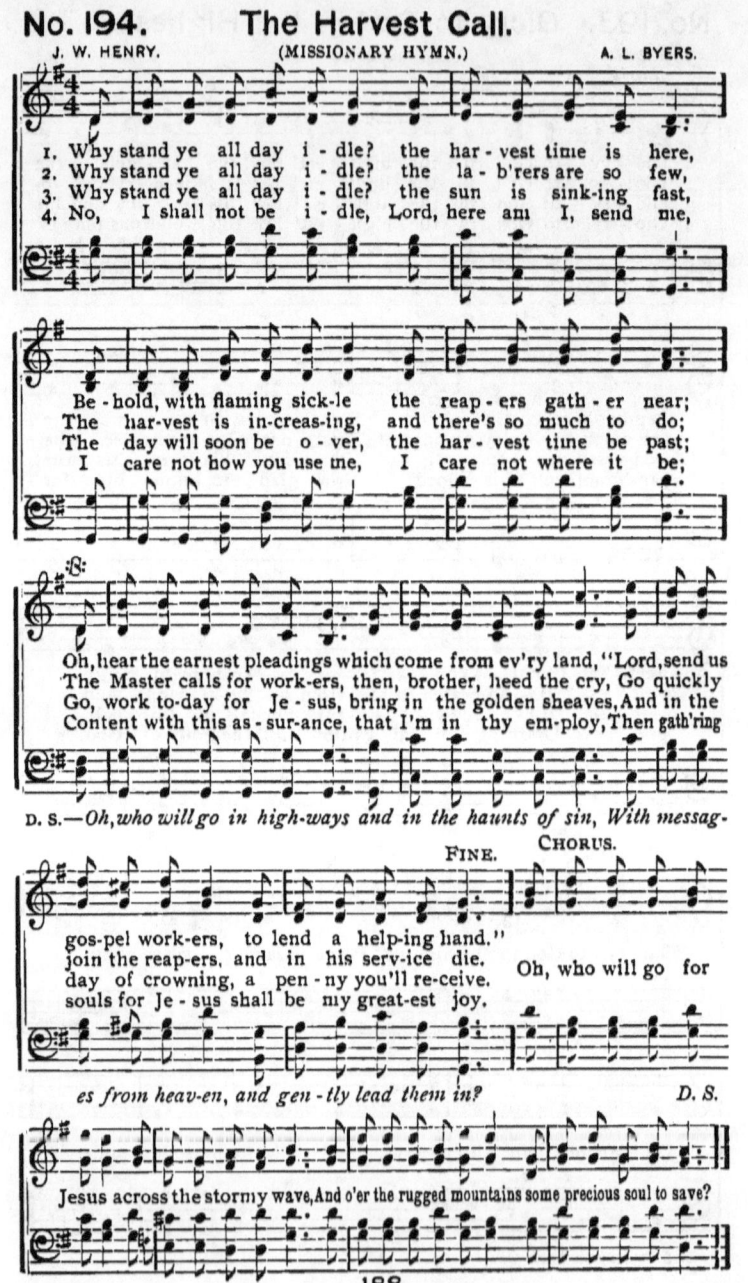

No. 198. Shall I Die Without a Savior?

B. E. W.
B. E. WARREN.

1. Shall I die with-out a Sav-ior? Shall I lose my precious soul?
2. Shall I die with-out a Sav-ior? Shall I hear his voice no more?
3. Shall I die with-out a Sav-ior? Per-ish when I see the light?
4. Shall I die with-out a Sav-ior? Per-ish just in sight of home?
5. Shall I die with-out a Sav-ior? And yet, hope to make a start?

Shall I cross death's chilly riv-er? Shall I miss yon brighter goal?
Shall I let my heart grow harder? Shut my-self from mercy's door?
Still neg-lect-ing, doomed forever— Banished to the dark-est night?
And be lost, yea, lost for-ev-er, Reach my aw-ful, fi-nal doom?
Still re-fus-ing him to en-ter, And thus tighter lock my heart?

CHORUS.

Shall I gain a home in heav-en? Shall I live in sin be-low?
Lose my crown, my soul and mansion, And go down to endless woe?

No. 199. Jesus the King.

EMMA I. COSTON.   A. L. BYERS.

1. Tho' kingdoms are ma-ny, and mas-ters are more, There's on-ly one
2. As way-far-ing soldiers we're marching a-long, Ac-cept-ing the
3. As chil-dren of God we are heirs with his Son, Brought nigh by the
4. As pil-grims and strangers we wait here be-low, We wor-ship King
5. As saints of Je-ho-vah, we run to and fro, De-liv-er his

King that gives life ev-er-more; His name, it is Je-sus, his
truth and re-ject-ing the wrong, Vic-to-rious in bat-tle, fair
blood of the Cru-ci-fied One; To him be our prais-es, a-
Je-sus, no oth-er we know; Tho' sin and con-fu-sion op-
mes-sage to both friend and foe; We her-ald the gos-pel and

prais-es we'll sing, We'll hon-or his name, for he is the King.
tro-phies to bring And cast at the feet of Je-sus, the King.
gain we will sing, All glo-ry to Je-sus, for he is the King.
pose, we will sing Our prais-es to Je-sus, for he is the King.
joy-ful-ly sing Our prais-es to Je-sus, for he is the King.

CHORUS.

I'm a child of the King, faith's off'ring I bring In hon-or to Je-sus, for he is the King.

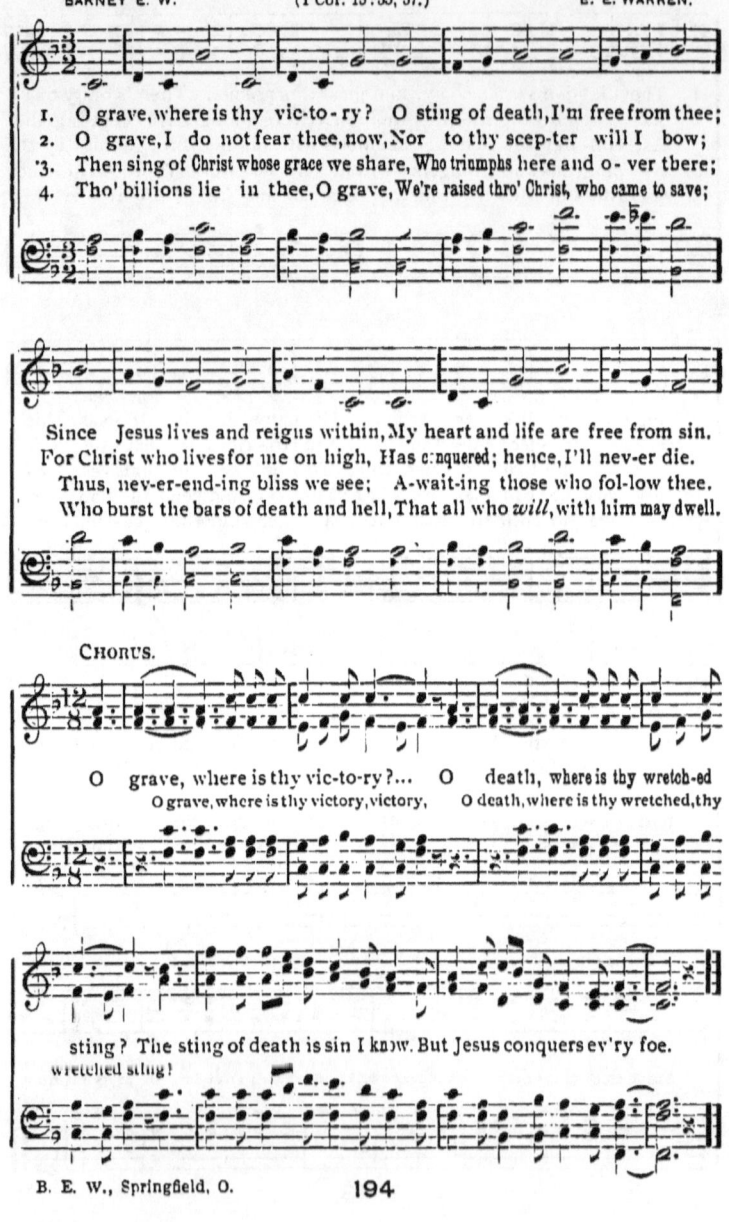

No. 201. Who Shall Dwell with Christ?

D. S. W.   (P's. 24:3,4.)   J. C. F. Har. by B. E. W.

1. Oh, who can stand the judgment day? None but the pure shall dwell with Christ.
2. Now, sinner, wake and turn to God, None but the pure shall dwell with Christ.
3. All ye that love this world of sin, None but the pure shall dwell with Christ.
4. You must be ho-ly, white as snow, None but the pure shall dwell with Christ.
5. Back slid-er, you must turn a-gain, None but the pure shall dwell with Christ.

Then, what, poor sinner, can you say, None but the pure shall dwell with Christ.
Ye lost, oh, flee to Jesus' blood, None but the pure shall dwell with Christ.
Think you that Christ will take you in? None but the pure shall dwell with Christ.
Or you can-not to heav-en go, None but the pure shall dwell with Christ.
Or you can-not in glo-ry reign, None but the pure shall dwell with Christ.

REFRAIN.

No, no, no, my Lord, None but the pure shall dwell with thee;

No, no, no, my Lord! None but the pure shall dwell with thee.

No. 202. He Shed His Blood for All.

W. G. SCHELL.   (MISSIONARY HYMN.)   W. G. S. Har. by B. E. W.

1. Fourteen hundred million souls, Standing near the final goal, Soon we'll
2. Ev-'ry sec-ond, sad to tell, Counts an-oth-er soul in hell,—Dreadful
3. Tho' a mill-ion be bro't in, There's a bill-ion yet in sin; Quick-ly
4. Can we tar-ry home for dross, While beholding such a loss? If we

see the aw-ful judgment on them fall; Must they tru-ly be con-signed
sight to see them bound in sin's dark pall. What in life we all may do,
bear the gos-pel message un-to all. Preach the word at a-ny cost,
can, from heaven's grace we'll surely fall. Quickly leave thy cottage door,

To the pit and there confined, Since the blessed Savior shed his blood for all.
Can but save a ver-y few, Yet the blessed Savior shed his blood for all.
For the world in sin is lost, Yet the blessed Savior shed his blood for all.
Spread the truth from shore to shore; For the blessed Savior shed his blood for all.

No. 203. Keep Me Near the Cross.

B. E. WARREN.   Air by S. L. SPECK. Har. by B. E. W.

1. Keep me near the cross, Keep me near the cross; Help me count all
2. Keep me near the cross, Keep me near the cross; Let life's foaming
3. Keep me near the cross, Keep me near the cross; I am free, O
4. Keep me near the cross, Keep me near the cross, While I rest in

Keep Me Near the Cross. Concluded.

else but dross, Keep me near the cross. Keep me near the cross,......
bil-lows toss, Keep me near the cross.
Lord, in thee, Keep me near the cross.
thee I'm blest, Keep me near the cross. Keep me near, yes, near the cross,

Keep me near the cross; All for Christ I suffered loss, Keep me near the cross.
Keep me near, yes, near the cross; Keep me near, yes, near the cross.

No. 204. O Precious Savior!

B. E. W.   B. E. WARREN.

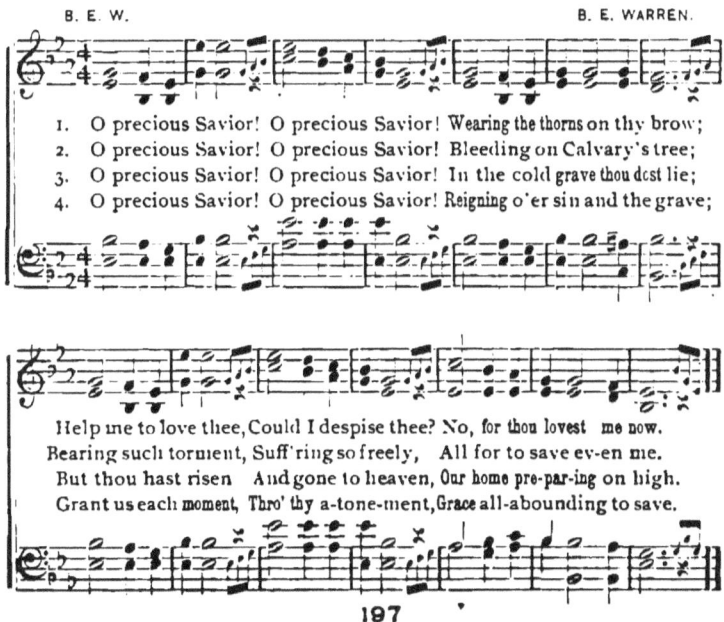

1. O precious Savior! O precious Savior! Wearing the thorns on thy brow;
2. O precious Savior! O precious Savior! Bleeding on Calvary's tree;
3. O precious Savior! O precious Savior! In the cold grave thou dost lie;
4. O precious Savior! O precious Savior! Reigning o'er sin and the grave;

Help me to love thee, Could I despise thee? No, for thou lovest me now.
Bearing such torment, Suff'ring so freely, All for to save ev-en me.
But thou hast risen And gone to heaven, Our home pre-par-ing on high.
Grant us each moment, Thro' thy a-tone-ment, Grace all-abounding to save.

No. 205. The Engrafted Word.

Words and Air by GEO. W. HOWARD. (Jas. 1:21.)   L. A. HOWARD. Harmonized.

1. Father, in us now re-veal-ing, The meek Spir-it of thy Son;
2. Jus-ti-fied by thy free Spir-it, Cleansed from ev-'ry guilt-y stain;
3. Sanc-ti-fied by God, the Father, Free from sense of in-bred sin;

In our souls and bod-ies feel-ing, Life a-new has just be-gun.
May we have thy word engrafted, Till it shines in all the same.
Now we feel the perfect cleansing, Just as pure as Christ within.

D. S.—Till we pass be-yond the por-tal, To our home so far a-way.

CHORUS.

Let the life of Je-sus tru-ly Dwell with-in us ev-'ry day,

No. 206. Kneeling in Prayer.

B. E. W.   (FAMILY PRAYER SONG.)   B. E WARREN.

Solemnly.

1. Now we come in thy name loving Christ, And we rest all agreed on thy word;
2. We are wait-ing before thee in pray'r, We are kneeling low down at thy feet;

Oh, thy promise ful-fill un-to us, Let each heart with de-vo-tion be stirred.
Oh, pre-pare us thy blessing to share, That each one of us may be complete.

No. 207. The Reeking Cross.

S. G. ODELL
J. C. FISHER.
Har. by A. L. BYERS.

1. See the reek-ing cross of Je-sus, Crim-son with his own life's blood;
2. Dreadful weight of guilt and anguish, Has-ten to the reek-ing cross;
3. Oh, his pre-cious blood that bought us! Oh, his pit - y for the lost!
4. Has-ten to him, sin-ner, has-ten! Heav'n conspires to make you blest;
5. Yield your heart and life to Je-sus, Free - ly he his grace will give;

Thus he died, lest we should perish, Wondrous love! thou Son of God.
Weight that on our souls had fal-len, But for his un-bound-ed love.
Can you slight his love, poor sin-ner, While so near the shelt'ring cross.
Fa-ther, Son and Spir - it call you; Come with all your woes oppress'd.
With him you shall reign in glo - ry, If for him on earth you live.

CHORUS.

He will save you, trembling sinner, Has-ten to the reek-ing cross;

Oh, be-lieve him, he will save you, Save you at the shelt'ring cross.

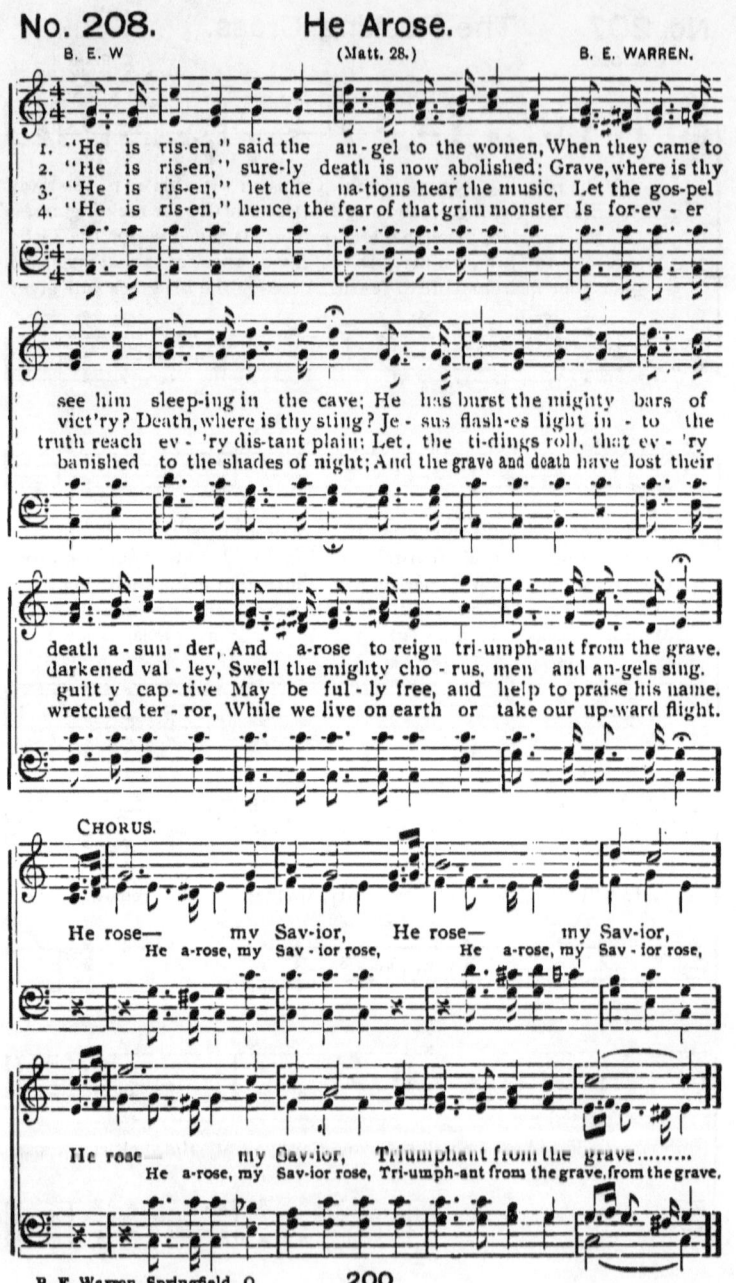

No. 209. Our Mother.

(Dedicated to the sacred Memory of our Mother.)

B. E. W.   B. E. WARREN.

1. Our mother is sleeping in Jesus to-day, Resting from earthly care, heavenly bliss to share; The angels of glory have borne her away, To dwell in that home over there.
2. She's gone from our circle, she'll never return, Gone where the angels dwell, safe from the pow'rs of hell; Our hearts are all broken and bleeding—we mourn—Dear mother, we love thee so well!
3. We hold thee in mem'ry the dearest of all— All of this world below, transient as falling snow; Tho' death's sable curtain between us did fall, We see thee wherever we go.
4. Her voice is now hushed, we shall hear it no more, Trembling with tearful eye, groaning with painful sigh, She's singing with angels on that happy shore, She's living there never to die.
5. Her last deeds of kindness are done for us here, But she is with the Lord, waiting her great reward; If we live for Jesus, we've nothing to fear, We'll meet her in holy accord.

CHORUS.

We weep not as those who are left without hope, For our sadness is turned into joy;
Because we'll soon rest with the happy and blest, In heaven where foes ne'er annoy.

B. E. Warren, Springfield, O.

No. 215. Come Out from Among Them.

B. E. W.   (2 Cor. 6:17.)   B. E. WARREN.

1. Have you heard the trumpet sounding? Have you heard the angel's call?
2. Sound the ti-dings o'er cre - a - tion, Let God's faithful children know,
3. Hear that voice from heaven, brother, Heed the warning, come to - day;
4. He has said, 'My people know me, And my voice they will o - bey;

Flee from sin and sect con-fus-ion, Come to Zi - on, one and all.
Sin-ful sects and all di - vis-ion, Sep - a - rate them here be-low.
Leave the names and creeds of Babylon, Take the ho - ly Bi - ble way.
So, if you are mine, you'll prove it, Just by do - ing what I say.'

CHORUS.

Come out from a-mong them, Come out from a-mong them,

Oh, do not par-take of her sins; Come out from a-mong them,

Come out from a-mong them, For her judgment already be - gins.

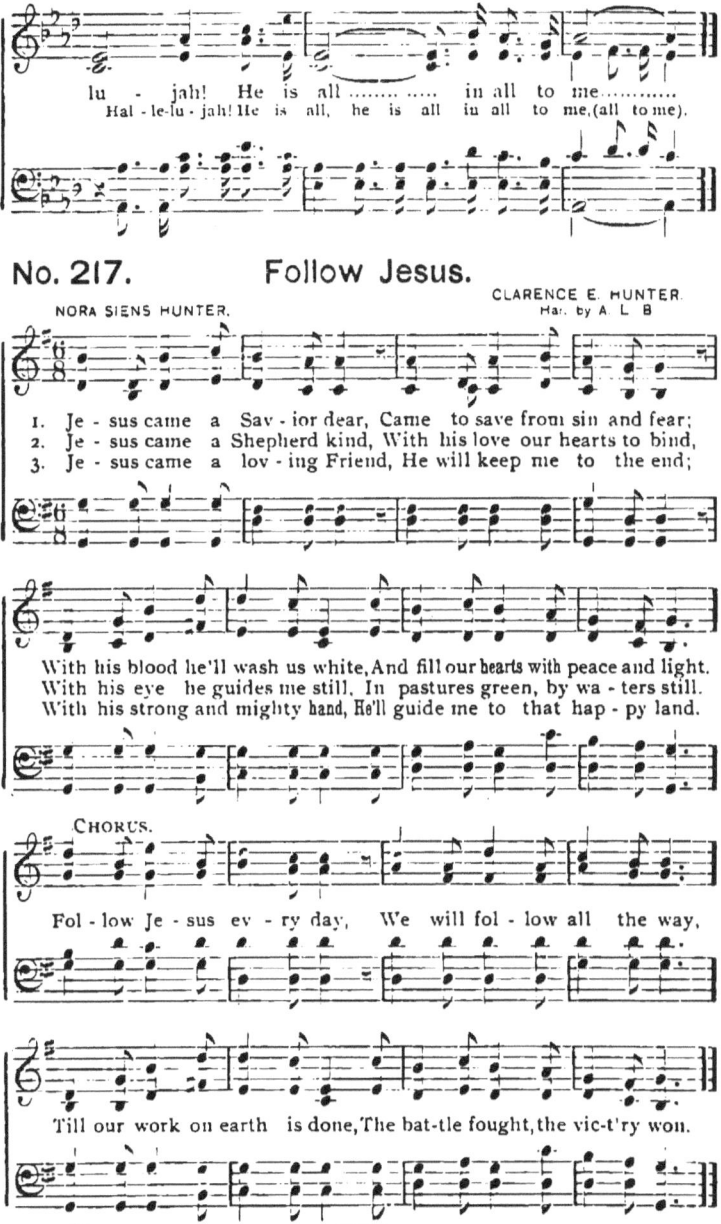

The Judgment Day. Concluded.

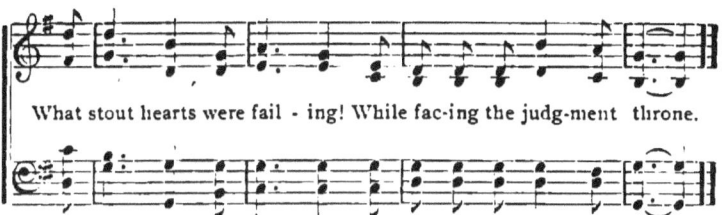

What stout hearts were fail - ing! While fac-ing the judg-ment throne.

5 Professors were there in confusion,
On their stilted self-righteousness too,
But ther filthy "old rags" of profession,
They found would not carry them thr.'.
And those who had crucified Jesus
Tho't they'd surely pass in all right,
But they were cast off on the left hand,
And sank into eternal night.

6 The souls that neglected salvation
And moral men vainly did try
To plead their excuse and profession:
"We hoped to be saved by and by;"

Thus stifling conviction and mercy,
A call from the regions on high
Came, startling, "'Tis death and the judgment!
Too late! your doom's sealed! you must die!"

7 The Christian was there in great boldness,
Awaiting his final reward,
All robed in the whiteness of Jesus,
Beholding the face of his Lord.
And then he heard gladly the tidings,
"Come, ye blessed, inherit for aye,
The kingdom and crown and your mansion,
And dwell in my presence alway."

No. 219. Morning Hymn.
Key E♭.

1 O God, inspire our morning hymn
Of love and gratitude;
Oh, bless the sacrifice we bring,
Thou source of every good.

CHORUS.

Touched by thy hand of love, we wake,
And rise from sweet repose;
Thy praise shall first the silence break,
Thy peace within us flows.

2 Thy miracle of love so sweet,
Preserved us all secure;
While helpless in unconscious sleep,
Thy presence kept us pure.

3 'Tis blest to rise, O Lord, and join
With nature's minstrelsy;
To hymn thy praise at early morn,
And offer thanks to thee.

4 Sweet morning is the time to pray,
How lovely and how meet,
To send our early thoughts away,
Up to the mercy seat.

5 The glorious sun has driven far,
The mystic shades of night;

So in our soul the Morning Star
Hath shed his wondrous light.
D. S. W.

No. 220. Full Salvation.
Key E♭.

1 Precious Savior, thou hast saved me,
Thine and only thine I am;
Oh! the cleansing blood has reached me,
Glory, glory to the Lamb!

CHO —Glory, glory. Jesus saves me,
Glory, glory to the Lamb!
Oh! the cleansing blood has reached me,
Glory, glory to the Lamb!

2 Long my yearning heart was trying
To enjoy this perfect rest;
But I gave all trying over,—
Simply trusting I was blest.

3 Trusting, trusting every moment,
Feeling now the blood applied;
Lying at the cleansing fountain,
Dwelling in my Savior's side.

4 Consecrated to thy service,
I will live and die with thee;
I will witness to thy glory,
Of salvation full and free.
L. M. ROUSE.

The Penitent's Plea. Concluded.

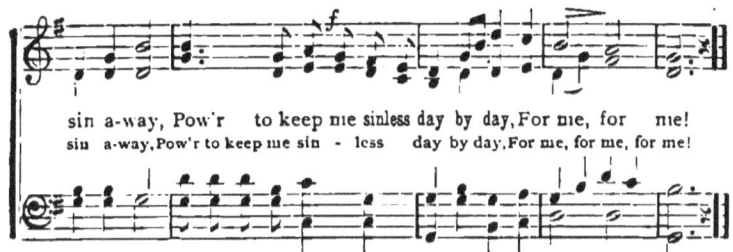

sin a-way, Pow'r to keep me sinless day by day, For me, for me!

No. 224. Key F.

1 We're a happy pilgrim band,
　Dwelling in the holy land,
With a shout of joy we upward run;
　For we've left the wilderness,
　And have entered holiness
Thro' the blood of God's beloved Son.

CHO.—Oh, its glory in my soul.
　Oh, its glory in my soul;
　For my Jesus dwells within,
　For my Jesus dwells within.

BASS.—Oh, its glory, glory, glory, yes,
　its glory in my soul;
　For my Jesus, oh, my blessed,
　loving Jesus dwells within.

2 In this land of corn and wine,
　We are happy all the time—
Oh, what flowing streams of perfect love—
　God himself is our delight,
　And we're walking in his light,
Pure as crystal, like his throne above.

3 Tho' we enter more and more,
　It is better on before,
Oh, the waves of glory still increase;
　Higher, higher we ascend,
　Yet we never see the end
Of this Beulah land of perfect peace.

4 Sing, oh, sing in sweet accord,
　The salvation of the Lord,
For he makes us whiter than the snow;
　Yes, we'll sing the jubilee,
　How the Son hath made us free,
And we triumph over every foe.

5 Ho, ye, sinners, come to-day,
　There is danger in delay;
Will you go to darkness and despair?

Oh, do turn away from sin,
And the Lord will take you in,
And his glory you may ever share.

6 And professors, where are you?
Are you holy through and through?
Are you living for the Lord alone?
　Oh, unless you're sanctified,
　You can never, never 'bide
In the presence of the heavenly throne.
　　　　　　　　　　D. S. W.

No. 225. Key F.

1 Sitting at the feet of Jesus,
　Oh, what words I hear him say!
Happy place, so near, so precious,
　May it find me there each day.
Sitting at the feet of Jesus,
　I would look upon the past,
For his love has been so gracious,
　It has won my heart at last.

2 Sitting at the feet of Jesus,
　Where can mortal be more blest?
There I lay my sins and sorrows,
　And when weary find sweet rest.
Sitting at the feet of Jesus,
　There I love to weep and pray,
While I from his fullness gather
　Grace and comfort every day.

3 Bless me, O my Savior, bless me,
　As I sit low at thy feet;
Oh, look down in love upon me,
　Let me see thy face so sweet.
Give me, Lord, the mind of Jesus,
　Keep me holy as he is.
May I prove I've been with Jesus,
　Who is all my righteousness.

No. 226.   Key A♭.

1 'Twas sung by the poets, foreseen in the Spirit,
A time of refreshing is near,
When creeds and divisions would fall to demerit,
And saints in sweet union appear.

CHORUS.

Oh, glory to Jesus, we hail the bright day,
And high on our banner salvation display,
The mists of confusion are passing away.

2 We stand in the glory that Jesus has given,
The moon, as the day-spring doth shine;
The light of the sun is now equal to seven,
So bright is the glory divine.

3 Now, filled with the Spirit, and clad in the armor
Of light, and omnipotent truth,
We'll testify ever, and Jesus we'll honor,
And stand from sin Babel aloof.

4 The prophet's keen vision, transpiercing the ages,
Beheld us to Zion return;
We'll sing of our freedom, tho' Babylon rages,
We'll shout as her city doth burn.

5 The fig tree is budding, the "evening" is shining,
We welcome the wonderful light;
We look for the Savior, for time is declining,
Eternity's looming in sight.

D. S. W.

No. 227.   Key G.

1 Will you come, will you come, with your poor broken heart,
Burdened and sin oppressed?
Lay it down at the feet of your Savior and Lord,
Jesus will give you rest.

REFRAIN.

Oh, happy rest, sweet, happy rest!
Jesus will give you rest,
Oh, why won't you come in simple, trusting faith?
Jesus will give you rest.

2 Will you come, will you come? there is mercy for you,
Balm for your aching breast;
Only come as you are and believe on his name,
Jesus will give you rest.

3 Will you come, will you come? you have nothing to pay;
Jesus, who loves you best,
By his death on the cross purchased life for your soul,
Jesus will give you rest.

4 Will you come, will you come? how he pleads with you now!
Fly to his loving breast,
And whatever your sin or your sorrow may be,
Jesus will give you rest.

From "Joy to the World," by per. J. R. Sweney.)

No. 228.   Key E♭.

1 Come, sinner, to the Living One,
He's just the same Jesus
As when he raised the widow's son,
The very same Jesus.

CHORUS.

The very same Jesus,
The wonder working Jesus; [same,
Oh, praise his name, he's just the
The very same Jesus.

2 Come, feast upon the "living bread,"
He's just the same Jesus
As when the multitudes he fed,
The very same Jesus.

3 Come, tell him all your griefs and
He's just the same Jesus [fears,
As when he shed those loving tears,
The very same Jesus.

4 Come unto him for clearer light,
He's just the same Jesus [sight,
As when he gave the blind their
The very same Jesus.

5 Calm 'midst the waves of trouble be,
He's just the same Jesus
As when he hushed the raging sea,
The very same Jesus.

6 Some day our raptured eyes shall
He's just the same Jesus; [see
Oh, blessed day for you and me!
The very same Jesus.

(Copyright, 1891, by Wm. J. Kirkpatrick. Used by per.)

No. 229. Key A♭.

1 Can I defeat my Savior's plan,
　Trample his mercy in the dust?
　Were I to act the part of a man,
　Could I but do what's right and just?

CHORUS.

　I will no longer doubt thee, O Lord,
　I will for ever stand on thy Word;
　I will believe and simply trust;
　Can I have faith? Yes, Lord, I must.

2 I will reject all doubts and fears,
　I will believe and simply trust;
　Thou hast said, "Cast on me thy cares,"
　Can I obey? Yes, Lord. I must.

3 Since I'm dependent, Lord, on thee,
　Why should I doubt thy saving grace?
　If by resisting, Satan must flee,
　Then I behold thy smiling face.

4 Shall I bring grief and sorrsw again,
　Into the heart of my dear Lord?
　No, I'll confess and honor his name,
　I will believe his precious word.
　　　　　　　　　　B. E. W.

No. 230.

1 Alas, and did my Savior bleed,
　And did my Sov'reign die?
　Would he devote that sacred head
　For such a worm as I?

CHORUS.

　Help me, dear Savior, thee to own,
　And ever faithful be;
　And as thou sittest on thy throne,
　Dear Lord, remember me.

2 Was it for crimes that I have done,
　He groaned upon the tree?
　Amazing pity, grace unknown,
　And love beyond degree!

3 But drops of grief can ne'er repay
　The debt of love I owe;
　Here, Lord, I give myself to thee,
　'Tis all that I can do.

No. 231. Key G.

1 If thou wilt know the fountain deep,
　Of sweet unbroken rest;
　The rest of faith thy soul shall keep,
　He that believes is ever blest.

CHORUS.

　Put on thy strength, O Zion rise,
　And fix thy trust above the skies;
　Move out on faith's almighty plain,
　Thro' him that loved us dare to reign.

2 The gift of faith no limit knows,
　Save God's unbounded word;
　It triumphs o'er its giant foes,
　And glorifies the blessed Lord.

2 Stay not in feeble unbelief,
　When God commands be strong;
　Be strong in him, the Word believe,
　And shout the overcomer's song.

4 I can do all in Jesus' name,
　Thus sings the faith of God;
　It sings and hills of trouble flee,
　It rides triumphant on the flood.
　　　　　　　　　　D. S. W.

No. 232. Key D.

1 Take my life and let it be
　Consecrated, Lord, to thee;
　Take my hands and let them move
　At the impulse of thy love.

CHORUS.

　Wash me in the Savior's precious blood,
　Cleanse me in its purifying flood; [be
　Lord, I give to thee my life and all to
　Thine henceforth eternally.

2 Take my feet and let them be
　Swift and beautiful for thee;
　Take my voice and let me sing
　Always, only for my King.

3 Take my lips and let them be
　Filled with messages for thee;
　Take my silver and by gold,—
　Not a mite would I with hold.

4 Take my moments and my days,
　Let them flow in endless praise;
　Take my intellect, and use
　Every pow'r as thou shalt choose.

5 Take my will and make it thine,
　It shall be no longer mine;
　Take my heart,—it is thine own,—
　It shall be thy royal throne.

6 Take my love,—my Lord, I pour
　At thy feet its treasured store;
　Take myself, and I will be
　Ever, only, all for thee.

(From "Glad Hallelujahs," by per. W. J. Kirkpatrick.)

No. 233. Key E♭.

1 Oh, now I see the cleansing wave,
  The fountain deep and wide;
  Jesus, my Lord, mighty to save,
  Points to his wounded side.

CHORUS.
The cleansing stream, I see, I see,
I plunge, and oh, it cleanseth me!
Oh, praise the Lord, it cleanseth me!
It cleanseth me, yes, cleanseth me.

2 I rise to walk in heav'n's own light,
  Above the world of sin, [white,
  With heart made pure and garments
  And Christ enthroned within.

3 Amazing grrce! 'tis heaven below
  To feel the blood applied;
  And Jesus, only Jesus know,
  My Jesus crucified.
  (By per. Mrs. J. F. Knapp.)

No. 234. Key A♭.

1 'Tis so sweet to trust in Jesus,
  Just to take him at his word;
  Just to rest upon his promise,
  Just to know, "Thus saith the Lord."

CHORUS.
Jesus, Jesus, how I trust him!
How I've proved him o'er and o'er!
Jesus, Jesus, precious Jesus!
Oh, for grace to trust him more!

2 Oh, how sweet to trust in Jesus,
  Just to trust his cleansing blood;
  Just in simple faith to plunge me
  'Neath the healing, cleansing flood.

3 Yes, 'tis sweet to trust in Jesus,
  Just from sin and self to cease;
  Just from Jesus simply taking
  Life and rest, and joy and peace.

4 I'm so glad I learned to trust thee,
  Precious Jesus, Savior, Friend;
  And I know that thou art with me,
  Wilt be with me to the end.
  (From "Songs of Triumph," by per. Wm. J. Kirkpatrick.)

No. 235. Key B♭.

1 Hear the voice of our Commander,
    Standing firm,
  Holy pilgrims, take the armor,
    Standing firm;
  Shod in gospel preparation,
  Sword and helmet of salvation,
  Meekly hold the true position,
    Standing firm.

CHORUS.
Fear not, brethren, firm and true,
  What-e'er thy foe may be;
Jesus fought the battle through,
  And gives to us the victory.

2 If it be thy lot to suffer,
    Standing firm,
  Vilest slander tongue can utter,
    Standing firm;
  Leap and shout, for then is given
  Greater thy reward in heaven,
  When the wicked far are driven,
    Standing firm.

3 In the time of sore temptation,
    Standing firm,
  Grace will be thy sure salvation,
    Standing firm;
  Virtue crown thy soul with honor,
  Sin resisted tempts no longer,
  Faith in conflict waxes stronger,
    Standing firm.

4 'Mid the battle's raging fury,
    Standing firm,
  Face the legions dark before thee,
    Standing firm;
  In the strength of our Redeemer,
  Make the pow'rs of hell surrender,
  Be a valiant overcomer
    Standing firm.
                        D. S. W.

No. 236. Key E.

1 In the rifted Rock I'm resting,
    Safely sheltered I abide;
  There no foes nor storms molest me
    While within the cleft I hide.

CHORUS.
Now I'm resting, sweetly resting
  In the cleft once made for me;
Jesus, blessed Rock of Ages,
  I will hide myself in thee.

2 Long pursued by sin and Satan,
    Weary, sad, I longed for rest;
  Then I found this heavenly shelter,
    Opened in my Savior's breast.

3 Peace which passeth understanding,
    Joy the world can never give,
  Now in Jesus I am finding;
    In his smiles of love I live.

4 In the rifted Rock I'll hide me,
    Till the storms of life are past;
  All secure in this blest refuge,
    Heeding not the fiercest blast.
                        MARY D. JAMES.

No. 237. Key A♭.

1 More about Jesus would I know,
More of his grace to others show;
More of his saving fulness see,
More of his love who died for me.

REFRAIN.
More, more about Jesus,
More, more about Jesus;
More of his saving fullness see,
More of his love who died for me.

2 More about Jesus let me learn,
More of his holy will discern;
Spirit of God, my teacher be,
Showing the things of Christ to me.

3 More about Jesus in his word,
Holding communion with my Lord,
Hearing his voice in every line,
Making each faithful saying mine.

4 More about Jesus, on his throne,
Riches in glory all his own;
More of his kingdom's sure increase,
More of his coming Prince of peace.

(From "Glad Hallelujahs," by per. J. R. Sweney.)

No. 238. Key B♭.

1 We are bound for the mansions of glory,
In that beautiful city of gold.
Where, beholding the face of our Savior,
It will fill us with rapture untold.

CHORUS.
When we get home, we'll shout and sing,
The praises of our Redeemer and King,
And make the heavenly arches ring
With the songs of home, sweet home.

2 'Tis the kingdom we have now within us,
It is comfort and peace and pure joy,
And a hope in our blessed Redeemer,
Which the world is to never destroy.

3 The Redeemer, with wonderful power,
Is now leading us on every day,
And if gladly we follow each moment,
He will keep us from wand'ring away.

4 We are dead to the world and its pleasure,
Our affections are centered above.
Where we own such a wonderful treasure,
'Tis a home in the city of love.
LUELLA B. HENRY.

No. 239. Key E♭.

1 When I was far away and lost,
Oh, 'tis wonderful,
That I was saved at such a cost!
Oh, 'tis wonderful!

CHORUS.
Oh, 'tis wonderful!
Oh, 'tis wonderful,
That Jesus gave his life for me!
Oh, 'tis wonderful!

2 I once was blind, but now I see;
Oh, 'tis wonderful!
Was bound by sin but now am free;
Oh, 'tis wonderful!

3 My guilt was all I had to bring;
Oh, 'tis wonderful!
Yet I was made his love to sing;
Oh, 'tis wonderful!

4 Come, sinner, now, and seek his
Oh, 'tis wonderful!   [grace,
And find in him a resting place;
Oh, 'tis wonderful!

No. 240. Key E♭.

1 Jesus and shall it ever be,
A mortal man ashamed of thee?
Ashamed of thee whom angels praise,
Whose glories shine thro' endless days?

CHORUS.
Ashamed of Jesus,
I never, I never will be,
For Jesus my Savior
Is not ashamed of me.

BASS.
Ashamed of Jesus, ashamed of Jesus,
I never, I never, I never will be,
For Jesus my Savior, for Jesus my Savior
Is not ashamed of me.

2 Ashamed of Jesus! sooner far,
Let evening blush to own a star;
He sheds the beams of light divine,
O'er this once darkened soul of mine.

3 Ashamed of Jesus! just as soon
Let midnight be ashamed of noon;
'Twas midnight with my soul till he,—
Bright Morning Star, bid darkness flee.

4 Ashamed of Jesus! that dear Friend,
On whom my hopes of heav'n depend!
No! when I blush, be this my shame;
I ever will revere his name.

5 Ashamed of Jesus! No, I say,
Since all my guilt he's washed away;
How could I be ashamed of him
Who saves and keeps me from all sin!

No. 241. Key F.

1 Oh, do not let the word depart,
And close thine eyes against the light;
Poor sinner, harden not your heart,
Be saved, oh, to-night.

CHO.—Oh, why not to-night?
Oh, why not to-night?
Wilt thou be saved?
Then, why not to-night?

BASS.
Why not to-night? why not to-night?
Why not to-night? oh, why not to-night?
Wilt thou be saved? wilt thou be saved?
Then why not, oh, why not to-night?

2 This world has nothing new to give,
It has no new, no pure delight;
Oh, try the life that Christians live.
Be saved, oh, to-night.

3 Our Lord in pity lingers still,
And wilt thou thus his love requite?
Renounce at once thy stubborn will,
Be saved, oh, to-night.

4 Our blessed Lord refuses none,
Who would to him their souls unite;
Believe in him, the work is done,
Be saved, oh, to-night.

No. 242. Key E♭.

1 My soul in trouble roamed
Upon a weary plain,
And, ever restless, longed
A perfect bliss to gain.

CHORUS.
I have found it, Lord, in thee,
An everlasting store
Of comfort, joy and bliss to me,
How can I wish for more?

2 Oppressed with guilt, and woe,
With fears of hell o'ercast,
My soul no comfort knew,
Until I came to Christ.

3 I bore within my breast
A deep and painful void;
I wanted inward rest,
And peace that would abide.

4 My foolish soul had thought
To fill itself with mold
From earthly mines, yet bought
No true and lasting gold.

5 All in this world is dross,
Its pleasures soon decay;
Its honors prove a snare,
Its treasures fly away.
D. S. W.

No. 243. Key A♭.

1 I am learning of my Savior,
Precious lessons every hour,
How the soul, which he has ransomed,
May be kept by mighty power.

CHORUS.
I am learning, I am learning,
Precious truths in Jesus' word;
I am learning, I am learning,
Of the lowly Lamb of God.

2 Learning more and more to love him,
Yielding all into his will,
While a joy beyond all utt'rance,
Thro' and thro' my soul doth thrill.

3 I am learning how to serve him
With my hands, my heart, my feet;
And each day my Master's service,
To my soul becomes more sweet.

4 I am learning how to trust him
With my life and for all things;
And my soul, filled with his glory,
In exceeding gladness sings.
GEORGIA C. ELLIOTT.

No. 244. Key E♭.

1 I am satisfied with Jesus,
His salvation is complete;
I am resting on his promise,
Calmly trusting, oh, how sweet!

CHORUS.
Hallelujah for the cleansing!
It has reached my inmost soul;
And the glory now is streaming
In my heart from sin made whole.

2 On the mountain, in the darkness,
With despondency and fear,
I was lost, but Jesus found me,
Now his love my heart doth cheer.

3 I am satisfied with Jesus,
In his love I now abide;
Oh, his sweet embrace doth shield us,
And no evil can betide.

4 Satisfied, oh, hallelujah!
I will praise his name alone;
His eternal peace is flowing
Thro' my heart, his royal throne.

5 Love's great wings are folded o'er us,
Peace which nothing can offend,
Passeth all our understanding,
Wondrous grace! it has no end.
B. E. WARREN.

No. 245.
TUNE:—"*I Am Trusting.*"

1 Savior, now I come to thee,
Weak and helpless from disease,
Asking thee to set me free,
Give me life and health and peace.

CHORUS.

I am trusting, Lord, in thee,
Dear Lamb of Calvary,
Humbly at thy cross I bow,
Jesus heals me, heals me now.

2 Break the strength of Satan's hand,
Speak this sore disease away,
For I know at thy command
Every power must obey.

3 Precious Savior, this I know,—
'Tis thy will to set me free;
On me, now this grace bestow,
As I claim my liberty.

4 Now I stand upon thy word,
Now the promise I believe;
It is mine, I take it, Lord,
Perfect healing I receive.
J. W. BYERS.

No. 246. Key A♭.

1 Down at the cross where my Savior died.
Down where for cleansing from sin I cried;
There to my heart was the blood applied,
Glory to his name.

CHORUS.

Glory to his name,
Glory to his name, [applied,
There to my heart was the blood
Glory to his name.

2 I am so wondrously saved from sin,
Jesus so sweetly abides within;
There at the cross where he took me in,
Glory to his name.

3 O precious fountain that saves from sin,
I am so glad I have entered in; [clean,
There Jesus saves me and keeps me
Glory to his name.

4 Come to the fountain so rich and sweet,
Cast thy poor soul at the Savior's feet;
Plunge in to-day and be made com-
Glory to his name. [plete,
E. A. HOFFMAN.

No. 247. Key G.
TUNE:—"*Beulah Land.*"

1 Why should a doubt or fear arise,
As this poor little all of mine,
I lay a living sacrifice,
All on the altar, Christ divine.

CHORUS.

I'm fully thine, yes, wholly thine,
All on the altar, Christ divine,
The word of Jesus I believe,
The Sanctifier I receive;
All on the altar I abide,
And Jesus says I'm sanctified.

2 Ah, not a moment more I'll doubt,
And not a moment longer wait;
He shed his blood to sanctify,
He suffered death without the gate.

3 By faith I venture on his word,
My doubts are o'er, the vict'ry won,
He said the altar sanctifies,
I just believe him and 'tis done.

4 Thro' all my soul I feel his pow'r,
And in the precious cleansing wave
I wash my garments white this hour,
And prove his utmost pow'r to save.

No. 248. Key D♮.

1 I've found my Lord and he is mine,
He won me by his love;
I'll serve him all my years of time,
And dwell with him above.

CHORUS.

His yoke is easy, his burden is light,
I've found it so, I've found it so;
His service is my sweetest delight,
His blessings ever flow.

2 No other Lord but Christ I know,
I walk with him alone;
His streams of love forever flow
Within my heart, his throne.

3 He's dearer to my heart than life,
He found me lost in sin;
He calmed the sea of inward strife,
And bid me come to him.

4 My flesh recoiled before the cross,
And Satan whispered there:
"Thy gain will not repay the loss,
His yoke is hard to bear."

5 I've tried the road of sin and found
Its prospects all deceive;
I've proved the Lord, and joys abound,
More than I could believe.
D. S. W.

INDEX.

TITLES IN ITALICS; FIRST LINES IN ROMAN.

A

	No.
A Better Time is Coming	2
A Better Land	76
Abiding and Confiding	112
A friendless prisoner	142
A Happy Band	186
A Heaven is Here	70
All in Jesus as our Savior	47
All to thee, O Savior mine	135
Alas and did my Savior	230
Anointed	91
Anywhere with Jesus I can	59
A Prayer in Song	98
Are you of the few?	108
Are you saved from sin to-day?	136
Are you building on the Rock	65
Around the throne of God in heav'n	114
A Song of Praise	133
Ask and it shall be given you, brother	46
As I travel this world over	87
A sinner once to Jesus came	152
Asleep with Jesus, oh, how sweet	212
A terrible scene is before me	218
A wonderful Savior is Jesus my Lord	86

B

	No.
Be Ready, All	97
Be Strong and True	210
Beautiful robes so white	14
Beyond where Kedron's waters	37
Beyond this world of toil and care	111
Beautiful Christ, a Savior true	116
Be strong and valiant for the truth	210
Biblical Trace of the Church	20
Blessed Spirit for the asking	91
Blessed assurance, Jesus is mine	95
Blest was the hour that heavenly fire	103
Brighter days are sweetly dawning	1
Buried with Jesus	176
By the grace of God I am saved to-day	45

C

	No.
Calvary	181
Cast your care on Jesus, trust him now	21
Cast thy cares upon the Savior	123
Can I defeat my Savior's plan	229
Christian, gird the armor on	184
Christ is All	28
Christ in Gethsemane	37
Church of God, thou spotless virgin	197
Clouds are enfolding that gather	153
Come, Sinner, Come	9
Come, sinner, to the Living One	228
Complete in Christ	15
Come Jesus, Reign in Me	121
Come, While He is Calling	183
Come Out from Among Them	205
Come, poor sinner, come to Jesus	25
Come, my child, for I will teach thee	40
Come, prodigal child, to your Father	53
Come, all ye broken hearted	64
Come home, poor sinner, why longer roam	88
Come, little children, to Jesus	109
Come and give your heart to Jesus	115
Come, poor sinner, Christ is waiting	78

D

	No.
Dear friends, we have precious tidings	161
Defeat the Devil	136
Dear ones, are you saved from sin to-night	9
Do you love the world in its pomp	17
Do you triumph O my brother	124
Don't resist the Holy Spirit	102
Down at the cross where my Savior	246
Down in the Licensed Saloon	69
Down in the Garden	93

E

	No.
Endearing Lord	55
Ever Lead Me	157

F

	No.
Farewell to Sin	172
Farewell, dear friends, a long farewell	158
Father, in us now revealing	205
Floating Down the Stream	154
Follow Jesus	217
Fourteen hundred million souls	202
For perfect love I long have groaned	121

G

	No.
Gather Them Home Above	89
Glory to God in the highest	193
Good News to All	161
Go forth ye messengers of light	26

H

	No.
Hallelujah! what a thought	216
Happy Little Saints	122
Hark, dear sinner, don't you hear	24
Hark, I hear hope sweetly singing	143
Have you heard the joyful sound	62
Have you ever heard of Jesus	79
Hear the voice of our Commander	235
He Arose	208
He Answered Never a Word	142
He Hideth My Soul	86
He is Just the Same To-day	79
He is Waiting	25
He Shed His Blood for All	202
Hear the tidings loud and clear	54
He is risen said the angel to the women	208
Hid Away With Jesus	12
Holy Bible, how I love it!	147
Hope of the Righteous	111
Hope	177
How firm a foundation, ye saints	139
How can I please my Lord the most?	33
How safe is the soul that abides	131
Hurry and Tell Him	46
Humility, thou secret vale	67
Hushed by the shadows dark and drear	93

I

	No.
I am learning of my Savior	243
I Am from Sin Set Free	84
I Am Healed	173
I am free, the Lord hath saved me	127
I am only a little sailor	148
I am satisfied with Jesus	244
I am going to a home	76
I can hear my Savior calling	51
I entered once a home of care	28
If, dear sinner, you are longing	183
If You Will	22
If thou wilt know the fountain deep	231
I have left all sin's dominion	30
I have a home prepared for me	50
I hear my Savior saying	52
I have learned the wondrous secret	112
I have longed for the bliss of pardon	138
I'll Go With Him All the Way	51
I'll Enter the Open Door	138
I love to serve my Jesus, a priv'lege	221
I'll rise at early morning hour	99
I know my Jesus saves me, he heals	185
I Know My Name is There	163
I Must Tell Jesus	189
I'm on the road to heaven	3
I'm hid away with Christ in God	12
I'm never lonely any more	38
I'm satisfied with Jesus, he's everything	146
I'm in the Lord's sacred pavilion	73

INDEX.

Title	No.
I'm kneeling at the mercy seat	145
I'm redeemed, I'm redeemed from	60
In the awful day that's coming	97
I Never Shall Forget	126
In the Hollow of His Hand	30
In Jesus Christ I am complete	15
In the land of Galilee	32
In the cleft'd Rock I hide	178
In Jesus I've found a sweet rest	104
In faith she touched the hem of his	127
In the rifted Rock I'm resting	236
I ought to love my Savior, he loved	66
It is time to be thinking of heaven	70
I've Touched the Hem of His Garment	125
I've found my Lord and he is mine	14
I Will Guide Thee	40
I Will, I Will	7
I wonder if mother is praying for me	41

J

Title	No.
Jesus, and shall it ever be	240
Jesus, Thy Blood and Name	31
Jesus Saves from Sin To-day	54
Jesus Heals	62
Jewels	90
Jesus Will Do the Same for Thee	152
Jesus is Pleading for Thee	171
Jesus the King	196
Jesus is my Shepherd, so kind	62
Jesus came a Savior dear	217
Jesus, thy blood, thy precious blood	31

K

Title	No.
Keep me near the cross	203
Keep me near thee, blessed Jesus	27
Kneeling in Prayer	206

L

Title	No.
Leaning on the arms of Jesus	77
Lead me gently by thy hand, Savior	137
Let the gates of praise be open	133
Let worldly minds the world pursue	84
Little Pilgrims	148
Lost Forever	170
Love is Freedom's Law	100
Lo! heaven now opens to rapturous	46
Loving Savior, hear my cry	155

M

Title	No.
Many called, but few are chosen	108
Mercy is Calling for Thee	18
Meditation	149
Mighty to Keep	221
Mother is Praying for Me	44
Mother	87
Mother Has Gone Home	202
Morning Hymn	219
More about Jesus	217
My Jesus, I love thee	107
My days are swiftly passing by	35
My beloved is so fair	63
My name is in the book of Life	163
My soul in trouble roamed	242

N

Title	No.
Near the End	99
Now is the precious seed-time	11
Now we come in thy name	206

O

Title	No.
O blessed Lamb of God, so dear	181
O Christ divine	55

Title	No.
O do not let the word depart	241
O God, inspire our morning hymn	219
Oh, Give Your Heart to Jesus	10
Oh, Gather the Harvest In	58
Oh, Thos Blessed, Holy Rest	63
Oh, grave, where is thy victory?	200
Oh, why should I be lost	213
Oh, will you count the cost to-day	7
Oh, we are saved in Jesus' blood	13
Oh, why should I be idle	57
Oh, come to the Savior, thou poor	74
Oh, how weary and sad	101
Oh, shall I go to heaven and wear	106
Oh, who can stand the judgment day?	201
Oh, worship God the Father	117
Oh, precious Savior	204
Oh, the cross, the paecious cross	118
Oh, what will you do with Jesus	129
Oh, we love the children's meeting	144
Oh, drink of the river of pleasure	156
Oh, scatter seeds of loving deeds	43
Oh, Jesus, Lord, my life, my way	195
Oh, now I see the cleansing wave	233
Oh, Lord, Thou Healest Me	151
Oh, love divine unfathomed	100
O mourner in Zion	184
On To Victory	188
On the Rock	65
Only one narrow way, "I am the way"	182
Open Wide the Door	5
O Save Me at the Cross	155
O sinner, do no longer the downward	10
O sweet will of God	187
Our Needs Supplied	24
Out on this dark world	157
Our God is love, the angels know	130
Our mother is sleeping in Jesus to-day	209

P

Title	No.
Peace	214
Perishing souls at stake to-day	162
Plunge into the Fountain	80
Precious Home of Rest	75
Praise the Lord	117
Press the Battle On	195
Praise the Lord! there's sunlight in my	42
Press on, my brother, sister	61
Praise God for the Bible	71
Precious Savior, thou hast saved me	220

R

Title	No.
Rays of Hope	96
Reigning in this Life	124
Room at the cross for a trembling soul	105
Rush to the Rescue	210

S

Title	No.
Satisfied With Jesus	146
Savior hear me while before thy feet	223
Savior, thou art life to me	98
Savior, now I come to thee	245
See the dear children around you to-day	89
Seeds of Promise	43
See the great king of Babel	134
See the reeking cross of Jesus	207
See the storm raging in fury to day	211
Showers Are Falling	153
Shall I Miss It?	196
Shall I die without a Savior, shall I	198
Shall my soul ascend with rapture	56
Since the Comforter Has Come	38
Sinner, Christ is Waiting	78
Sinner, hark! the Savior's calling	5
Sing about Jesus, who died to save	132

INDEX.

Title	No.
Sitting at the feet of Jesus	225
Something for Children to Do	128
Some day when God's sweet Spirit	23
Sometimes I'm tried with toil and	222
Soon we'll lay our burdens down	21
Songs of victory bringing unto the Lord	34
Sowing the tares when it might have been	85
Some people may forget, they say	126
Step Out On the Promise	184
Sweet Haven of Love	140
Sweet Rest in Jesus	104
Sweet peace is flowing	214
Sweet rest in Jesus, home of the	75

T

Title	No.
Table Hymn	120
Take my life and let it be	232
Tell me of Jesus	16
The Evening Light	1
Then What Will Your Harvest Be?	11
The Onward March	13
The Love of God	19
The Wandering Exile	29
The City of Light	39
The Penitent's Plea	223
The All-Cleansing Fountain	41
The Precious Sunlight	42
The White Horse Cavalry	48
The Ninety-Nine	49
The Last Hymn	56
The Golden Harvest	57
There's a Mercy in the Savior	64
The Pilgrim's Confidence	81
The Sea of Glass	91
The Prodigal's Return	101
The Starless Crown	106
The Cross	118
Thy will be done, thy will	119
Thy will alone, dear Lord	180
That Wicked One Toucheth Him Not	131
The Hand of God on the Wall	134
That Happy World Above	141
The Children's Meeting	144
The Christian's Guide	147
The River of Pleasure	156
The Faithfulness of God	168
The Valley of Judgment	174
The Church Triumphant	175
The Clefted Rock	178
The Valley of Decision	179
The Bondage of Love	187
There's a theme that is sweet to my	4
The love of God flows deep and wide	19
The church of the morning bright	20
There's a promise divine in the Bible	29
There's a city of light 'mid the stars	39
There's a fountain opened	41
The ninety-nine within the fold	49
The hour of my departure	72
There are some rays of hope divine	96
There's only One whose pity falls	110
There is something for children to do	128
The world all around has no harbor	140
There's a happy world above	141
There's a peaceful valley of decision	179
The kingdoms are many	199

Title	No.
Thy Precious Will	180
That's Enough for Me	194
The Harvest call	195
The Engrafted Word	201
The Judgment Day	213
There is a happy band on earth	186
This Jesus	190
The Reeking Cross	207
'Tis Better Felt than Told	103
Time moves on with solemn footsteps	99
Time onward flows like a river	113
'Tis so sweet to trust in Jesus	234
To Be Lost in the Night	74
To the cross, Christian soldier	83
Trust and Obey	6
'Twas Love that Found Out Me	150
'Twas sung by the poets	226
Two little hands are sweetly folded	159

U

Title	No.
Under His Wings	73

V

Title	No.
Victory	216

W

Title	No.
Walking with Jesus	35
Wash me in thy blood divine	80
Walking thro' life's dark, shady valley	81
We Shall Run and Not Be Weary	165
We will work for Jesus	36
We Shall Meet	158
We're a happy pilgrim band	224
We're living in the end of time	58
We are bound for the mansions of glory	238
We are floating down the stream	154
What a Kingdom	4
What will You Do with Jesus?	129
When I was far away and lost	239
Why should a doubt or fear	247
Who will Suffer with Jesus?	160
Whiter than Snow	169
Who Shall Dwell with Christ?	201
Whosoever Will	213
Where is my wayword boy to-night?	192
When we walk with the Lord	6
Where shall I spend my eternity?	8
What Hast Thou Done for Me?	68
Where is my wand'ring boy to-night?	69
Who will suffer with the Savior?	160
What will you give in exchange for	196
Without Spot and Blameless	92
Will You Come?	115
Will you come, will you come?	227
Will you come and be free from	18

Y

Title	No.
Yes, I Will Please Jesus	33
You may know this day that your sins	22

Z

Title	No.
Zion's Onward March	32

MEREDITH, MUSIC PRINTER, CHICAGO.